Artificial Intelligence and Scientific Method

WITHDRAWN

Artificial Intelligence and Scientific Method

DONALD GILLIES

OXFORD UNIVERSITY PRESS
1996

Oxford University Press, Walton Street, Oxford OX2 6DP

Oxford New York

Athens Auckland Bangkok Bombay
Calcutta Cape Town Dar es Salaam Delhi
Florence Hong Kong Istanbul Karachi
Kuala Lumpur Madras Madrid Melbourne
Mexico City Nairobi Paris Singapore
Taipei Tokyo Toronto

and associated companies in
Berlin Ibadan

Oxford is a trade mark of Oxford University Press

Published in the United States
by Oxford University Press Inc., New York

British Library Cataloguing in Publication Data
Data available

Library of Congress Cataloging in Publication Data
Gillies, Donald, 1944–
    Artificial intelligence and scientific method / Donald Gillies.
    Includes bibliographical references and index.
    1. Artificial intelligence. 2. Science—Philosophy. I. Title.
    Q335.G54 1996 006.3—dc20 95-26846

ISBN 0–19–875158–3
ISBN 0–19–875159–1 (pbk.)

10 9 8 7 6 5 4 3 2 1

Typeset by Graphicraft Typesetters Ltd., Hong Kong
Printed in Great Britain
on acid-free paper by
Biddles Ltd., Guildford and King's Lynn

To Grazia and Mark

Preface

Remarkable advances have taken place in the field of artificial intelligence (AI) in the last twenty to thirty years. One of the aims of this book is to introduce the reader to some of these. It should be stressed that I am not attempting a comprehensive account. A better feeling for artificial intelligence will be obtained by considering a few examples in some detail than by a broad but superficial survey. I have accordingly selected just two topics for consideration. These are (i) machine learning in the Turing tradition and its link with expert systems research; and (ii) the development of logic programming and its connection with non-monotonic logic. In describing these areas, I have tried to avoid as much as possible the use of any technical or mathematical formulations, so that the accounts should be comprehensible to anyone with an interest in these matters. Only at one point in Chapter 4, when I was discussing some problems about translating from one logical system to another, did I have to break this rule and presuppose some technical results in logic. However, the relevant section (4.3) is marked with an asterisk, and can be omitted without losing the general thread of the argument. Yet, although I have eschewed the use of technicalities, I have tried to make my account as accurate as possible in order to convey some idea of how these AI systems actually work and how they were developed. An AI system can, all too easily, seem like a mysterious black box. Only by gaining some understanding of what goes on in the box is it possible to form a judgement about the significance of what has been achieved.

This brings me to the second aim of the book, which is to examine the implications of these advances in AI for philosophy, and particularly for the study of scientific method (including logic). These implications are, in my view, very far-reaching, and the recent results in artificial intelligence quite often cast a new and unexpected light on old philosophical problems, and on long-standing philosophical debates. The first such philosophical question to be considered is a debate about the nature of scientific method, which could be called *the inductivist controversy*. This controversy has been carried on for many years between *inductivists*, whose viewpoint goes back to Sir

Preface

Francis Bacon, and *falsificationists*, whose champion was Sir Karl Popper. The controversy is described in Chapter 1. In Chapter 2 an account of some recent results in machine learning is given, and then the consequences of these results for the inductivist controversy are explored in Chapter 3. Chapter 4 contains a description of logic programming, and this is then related to long-standing debates about the foundations of logic. An attempt is then made in Chapter 5 to integrate the results of Chapters 1, 2, 3, and 4 in a consideration of whether it is possible to have inductive as well as deductive logic, and, if so, what form inductive logic should take. As in my treatment of artificial intelligence, I have not presupposed any technical knowledge of logic or philosophy (except in Section *4.3), and have tried, as far as possible, to explain all the issues involved accurately but informally.

While developments in artificial intelligence certainly have implications for philosophy, it is also true that philosophy has implications for artificial intelligence. Once again I will not attempt a comprehensive survey of this side of the question, but rather concentrate on a single example—the example which has provoked more discussion than any other. Some of the most famous results in logic in the twentieth century are Gödel's incompleteness theorems, the proofs of which were published in 1931. Now some thinkers (notably Lucas, Penrose, and Gödel himself) have argued that these theorems of logic show that there is a limit to what can be achieved by artificial intelligence, and that the human mind can, in some respects at least, go beyond anything which could ever be done by a digital computer. In Chapter 6 I give an informal exposition of Gödel's incompleteness theorems, and then a full discussion of their implications for artificial intelligence. In the course of this discussion, it becomes natural to consider anxieties caused by the development of powerful computers. Is it altogether wise for human beings to create machines which might be more intelligent than themselves? Could mankind be surrendering its intellectual superiority to its creations? These are certainly disquieting questions, and worthy of careful consideration.

Donald Gillies

Department of Philosophy
King's College London
July 1995

Acknowledgements

I should like to begin by thanking the two friends of mine (Roberto Garigliano and Peter Gibbins) who first aroused my interest in artificial intelligence. Both had started as philosophers, but both changed to the AI field. Roberto Garigliano is now designing a system for natural language processing at the University of Durham, while Peter Gibbins is Head of Information Technology Research at the Sharp Laboratories of Europe. Each independently told me that advances in artificial intelligence were highly relevant to the philosophical problems on which I was working, and each urged me to take an interest in it. When I did so, I found that what they said was quite true, and indeed this book is an argument in favour of the accuracy of their viewpoint.

When I began studying artificial intelligence, I was very fortunate to have the opportunity of participating in two interdisciplinary projects in the field, and thus could learn something of the subject in a 'hands-on' fashion. The first of these projects was with my brother (Duncan Gillies) and Enrique Sucar. The general aim was to implement an expert system for providing diagnostic advice during colon endoscopy, and the three of us worked together on the question of how probability should be introduced into the system. We eventually came up with a technique which involved objective probabilities and a testing methodology, and which was published in *Artificial Intelligence* in 1993. The second project was a three-year (1990–3) SERC-financed project called the Rule-Based Systems Project. This involved Dov Gabbay and Tony Hunter from Imperial College, Stephen Muggleton and Ashwin Srinivasan, who were first at the Turing Institute in Glasgow and then at Oxford University, and James Cussens and me at King's College London. The aim of the project was to integrate non-monotonic logic (Imperial), machine learning (Turing/Oxford), and probability and confirmation theory (King's) to produce an improved rule-discovery system. The project also benefited from the participation of Ed Babb from ICL. I would like to say what a pleasure it was working on these projects, and to thank all those involved from whom I learnt so much about artificial intelligence and its possible applications. I should also like

Acknowledgements

to thank the SERC for its financial support of the second project (Grant GR/G 29854).

While work on these projects provided me with a background in artificial intelligence, I also received a great deal of assistance from the AI community on the various chapters. Donald Michie and Stephen Muggleton read over the first draft of Chapter 2 and suggested many improvements and further references. Similar help was given by Dov Gabbay and Bob Kowalski on Chapter 4, and by James Cussens and Tony Hunter on Chapter 5. The book is interdisciplinary in character, and I also received a great deal of useful criticism and advice from the philosophy community. Early versions of Chapters 4 and 6 were read at the philosophy department's weekly seminar at King's College London, and this gave rise to many useful comments, including several relating to technical aspects of PROLOG! In this connection I would like particularly to thank James Hopkins, Moshé Machover, and Mark Sainsbury, whose observations led to significant changes in the text. Among other things, Moshé Machover pointed out the relevance of Gödel's translations between classical and intuitionistic logic for the argument of Chapter 4. Charles Chihara, Wolfram Hinzen, and John Lucas were kind enough to read the first draft of Chapter 6 and offer detailed comments, several of which were incorporated into the final version of the chapter.

Finally I would like to acknowledge my gratitude to my old teacher Sir Karl Popper, who unfortunately died in September 1994 just as this book was nearing completion. As the reader will see, I think that the recent results in artificial intelligence do necessitate the revision of some of Sir Karl's views on induction, but this is not in any way to question the importance of his work in this field, which has stimulated so many, including myself, to take an interest in the problems connected with probability, induction, and confirmation. Moreover, although some of Sir Karl's ideas have been called into question by artificial intelligence, others have proved extremely valuable and stimulating for AI research.

Contents

Contents

... the art of discovery may advance as discoveries advance.

(Bacon, *Novum Organum*, 1620)

... and in his subsequent design for an Analytical Engine Mr. BABBAGE has shown that material machinery is capable, in theory at least, of rivalling the labours of the most practised mathematicians in all branches of their science. Mind thus seems able to impress some of its highest attributes upon matter, and to create its own rival in the wheels and levers of an insensible machine.

(Jevons, *On the Mechanical Performance of Logical Inference*, 1870)

1 The Inductivist Controversy, or Bacon versus Popper

THE aim of this book is to examine the interaction between theories of scientific method (including logic) and developments in the field of artificial intelligence (AI) which have taken place in the last twenty to thirty years. The first topic I will discuss is the relationship between a long-standing dispute concerning scientific method (the *inductivist controversy*) and some recent results in machine learning. The present chapter will give an account of the debate between the inductivists, conveniently represented by Sir Francis Bacon, and the anti-inductivists, conveniently represented by Sir Karl Popper. It is a strange coincidence that this *intellectual* dual should be conducted between two English knights! As far as the present chapter is concerned, I will expound the controversy using the standard methods of history and philosophy of science.[1] In the next chapter (Chapter 2), I will give an account of some relevant results from the development of machine learning in the Turing tradition. Then, in Chapter 3, I will consider how these results affect the inductivist controversy.

1.1. Bacon's Inductivism

The inductivist theory of scientific method (or inductivism) was first developed by Sir Francis Bacon (1561–1626). He expounded his theory in a number of works, but his most famous treatment of the question occurs in his *Novum Organum* of 1620, from which I will take quotations. Aristotle's collected writings on logic had been given the name *Organum* (literally 'tool'); thus Bacon's *Novum Organum*, or new *Organum* was intended to supersede Aristotle as an instrument of reasoning. Indeed Bacon believed that the new methods he proposed would be much more fruitful as regards the development of science and technology than the methods used by the ancient Greeks and medieval thinkers.

The basic idea of *inductivism* is simple enough. A scientist following this method should begin by making a large number of careful observations. Then, from this mass of data, laws should be extracted by a process known as *induction*. As his dates show, Bacon was a contemporary of Shakespeare (1564–1616). There is even a theory that Bacon wrote the plays of Shakespeare as well as his own philosophical works. Such a view is not taken seriously by scholars of the period, but it remains true that Bacon is contemporary with the greatest flowering of English literature, and that his literary style has a brilliance rarely to be found in philosophical writings. Thus he expounds his inductive theory of scientific method by means of the following memorable analogy:

Now other men, as well in ancient as in modern times, have in the matter of sciences drunk a crude liquor like water, either flowing spontaneously from the understanding, or drawn up by logic, as by wheels from a well. Whereas I pledge mankind in a liquor strained from countless grapes, from grapes ripe and fully seasoned, collected in clusters, and gathered, and then squeezed in the press, and finally purified and clarified in the vat. (Bacon 1620: 297–8)

Here the 'countless grapes . . . ripe and fully seasoned, collected in clusters' are the numerous observations from which juice for the wine of science is squeezed. But how exactly are scientific laws to be extracted from observations? Bacon makes it clear that the process is to be mechanical in character. As he says in the preface to his *Novum Organum*: 'There remains but one course for the recovery of a sound and healthy condition,—namely, that the entire work of the understanding be commenced afresh, and the mind itself be from the very outset not left to take its own course, but guided at every step: and the business be done as if by machinery' (Bacon 1620: 256).

In another of his striking analogies, Bacon compares the use of his new method for science with the use of a compass for drawing a circle. It is virtually impossible for even the most brilliant artist to draw a perfect circle free hand, but with a compass anyone can do it. There is one corollary of this which has caused dissatisfaction to many readers of Bacon. Bacon thinks that, if his mechanical method is followed, science will become a routine business, not requiring any special intelligence or ingenuity. As he says:

But the course I propose for the discovery of sciences is such as leaves but little to the acuteness and strength of wits, but places all wits and understandings nearly on a level. For as in the drawing of a straight line or a perfect circle, much depends on the steadiness and practice of the hand, if it be done by aim of hand only, but if with the aid of rule or compass, little or nothing; so is it exactly with my plan. (Bacon 1620: 270)

Later on, in Chapter 3, I will examine some of the details of Bacon's plan for making scientific discoveries mechanically. For the moment, I will simply observe that he refers to this process as *induction*. In the plan of the work he stresses his adherence to induction in the context of a characteristic polemic against the sterility of a portion of Aristotelian logic—the syllogism:

I therefore reject the syllogism . . . middle propositions . . . though obtainable no doubt by the syllogism, are, when so obtained, barren of works, remote from practice, and altogether unavailable for the active department of the sciences. . . . in dealing with the nature of things I use induction throughout . . . For I consider induction to be that form of demonstration which upholds the sense and closes with nature . . .
Hence it follows that the order of demonstration is likewise inverted. . . . my plan is to proceed regularly and gradually from one axiom to another, so that the most general are not reached till the last; and then when you do come to them you find them to be not empty notions, but well defined, and such as nature would really recognize as her first principles, and such as lie at the heart and marrow of things. (Bacon 1620: 249)

Bacon also stresses that he wants to change 'the form itself of induction', so that we can conveniently call his form of induction *Baconian* or *mechanical induction*. This type of induction is supposed to be a mechanical method of obtaining scientific laws from a large mass of data previously collected. But is there really such a method at all? Popper, for one, denied that such a method existed, and proposed a quite different account of how scientific research should be carried out. I will give a brief account of his views in the next section.

1.2. Popper's Falsificationism

Popper disagreed radically with all the views of Bacon which I have so far expounded.[2] To begin with Popper denied that there was such a thing as induction in the Baconian sense. Popper said very emphatically: 'Induction, i.e inference based on many observations, is a myth. It is neither a psychological fact, nor a fact of ordinary life, nor one of scientific procedure' (Popper 1963: 53). One of the key ideas of inductivism is that a scientist should make a large number of observations before attempting to infer a law or generalization. In other words, according to the inductivist, observation should precede theory. Popper argued against this that one cannot simply observe without a theoretical background. Here is how he put the argument:

The belief that science proceeds from observation to theory is still so widely and so firmly held that my denial of it is often met with incredulity. I have even been suspected of being insincere—of denying what nobody in his senses can doubt.

But in fact the belief that we can start with pure observations alone, without anything in the nature of a theory, is absurd; as may be illustrated by the story of the man who dedicated his life to natural science, wrote down everything he could observe, and bequeathed his priceless collection of observations to the Royal Society to be used as inductive evidence. This story should show us that though beetles may profitably be collected, observations may not.

Twenty-five years ago I tried to bring home the same point to a group of physics students in Vienna by beginning a lecture with the following instructions: 'Take pencil and paper; carefully observe, and write down what you have observed!' They asked, of course, *what* I wanted them to observe. Clearly the instruction, 'Observe!' is absurd. . . . Observation is always selective. It needs a chosen object, a definite task, an interest, a point of view, a problem. And its description presupposes a descriptive language, with property words; it presupposes similarity and classification, which in its turn presupposes interests, points of view, and problems. (Popper 1963: 46)

The same thing is supposed to apply even if we go right back to the beginnings of science or of an individual human life. Popper argued that something like modern science developed in ancient Greece through criticism and modification of an older mythological picture of the world. Newborn babies do not have blank minds, but inborn expectations as the result of genetic inheritance. However, as Popper pointed out, these expectations may be disappointed. The newborn child expects to be fed, but may be abandoned and starve.

These considerations led Popper to an account of scientific method which he presented as an alternative to inductivism. This is his theory of *conjectures and refutations* or *falsificationism*. On this account, science starts not with observations, as the inductivist claims, but with conjectures. The scientist then tries to refute (or falsify) these conjectures by criticism and testing (experiment and observations). A conjecture which has withstood a number of severe tests may be tentatively accepted, but only tentatively. It may break down on the very next test or observation. Any conjecture which has been refuted (or falsified) has to be given up, and scientists must try to rectify the situation either by modifying the old conjecture or by producing an entirely new one. The new, or modified, conjecture is then tested and criticized in its turn, so that science grows and progresses through a never-ending sequence of conjectures and refutations.

A further difference between Bacon and Popper concerns the question of how the conjectured theories are obtained. Bacon, as we have seen, hoped that scientific theories could be generated from observations by some kind of mechanical process, which 'places all wits and understandings nearly on a level'. Popper, on the other hand, thought that scientific theories (or at least the more interesting ones) are the product of the creative thinking of brilliant scientists such as Einstein who rely on some mysterious intuition which could perhaps be investigated by psychologists, but which is certainly not reducible to a logical procedure. Popper expounded this point of view as follows:

the work of the scientist consists in putting forward and testing theories. The initial stage, the act of conceiving or inventing a theory, seems to me neither to call for logical analysis nor to be susceptible of it. The question how it happens that a new idea occurs to a man—whether it is a musical theme, a dramatic conflict, or a scientific theory—may be of great interest to empirical psychology; but it is irrelevant to the logical analysis of scientific knowledge. . . . my view of the matter, for what it is worth, is that there is no such thing as a logical method of having new ideas, or a logical reconstruction of this process. My view may be expressed by saying that every discovery contains 'an irrational element', or 'a creative intuition', in Bergson's sense. In a similar way Einstein speaks of the 'search for those highly universal laws . . . from which a picture of the world can be obtained by pure deduction. There is no logical path', he says, 'leading to these . . . laws. They can only be reached by intuition, based upon something like an intellectual love ('Einfühling') of the objects of experience.' (Popper 1934: 31–2)

One of the interesting features of Popper's account is that it tends to reduce the gap often considered to exist between artists and scientists. Leading artists, such as the musicians and playwrights mentioned by Popper, are often thought to produce their works through a brilliant use of creativity, involving some mysterious, and perhaps irrational, intuition. Scientists, on the other hand, are often seen, perhaps under the influence of Bacon, as proceeding by more routine and mechanical methods. Popper, however, thinks that mysterious intuitions and creativity are just as necessary for the leading scientist as for the leading artist. Only by such means, he claims, can scientists produce the new conjectures which are needed for science to go forward.

These then are the principal points of difference between inductivism (Bacon), and falsificationism (Popper). How then are we to decide between the two views of scientific method? Of course the aim of the present book is to see what light recent results in artificial intelligence can cast on the controversy. However, rather than proceeding directly with this task, it will be useful to consider, in this first chapter of the book, a more traditional method of weighing the merits of competing theories in the philosophy of science. This is the method of analysing case histories of what is generally acknowledged to be good science, in order to see whether they fit the theories of science under consideration. In accordance with this approach, I will consider in the next two sections two famous episodes from the history of science to see what they tell us about the Bacon–Popper dispute. The examples chosen are of relevance to the material from artificial intelligence to be considered later on. Indeed the first example (that of Kepler's discovery of the laws of planetary motion) has been extensively discussed from the AI point of view by Simon and his group. We shall consider their views in Chapter 2. The second example (the discovery of the sulphonamide drugs) is related in some respects to the scientific use of the machine-learning program GOLEM, which we shall also consider in Chapter 2.[3]

1.3. Kepler's Discovery of the Laws of Planetary Motion

Kepler discovered three laws of planetary motion.[4] They can be stated as follows:

1. All planets move in ellipses, with the Sun at one focus.
2. The line joining a planet to the Sun sweeps out equal areas in equal times.

3. D^3/P^2 is constant for all planets, where D is the mean distance of the planet from the Sun, and P is its period.

The first two laws were published in his book *Astronomia Nova* (New Astronomy) in 1609, and the third in his book *Harmonices Mundi* (Harmony of the World) in 1619.

The events which led up to these discoveries were briefly as follows. Between 1576 and 1597 Tycho Brahe, a Danish astronomer, made a long series of careful observations of the heavens, particularly of the movements of the planets. The telescope had not then been invented, but Tycho Brahe's observations were the most accurate ever made with the naked eye. In 1597 he left Denmark to become Imperial Mathematician at the court of the Emperor Rudolf II in Prague. Here in 1600 he took on Johannes Kepler as his assistant.

Kepler set himself the task of working out the orbit of Mars from Tycho Brahe's data. At first he thought it would take him a week. In fact, he worked on the problem for over six years, before concluding that the orbit was an ellipse.

At first sight this appears to be a classic example of inductive method. Tycho Brahe painstakingly made a long series of careful observations of the planet Mars. Kepler in an equally careful and painstaking fashion inferred from these observations that the orbit of Mars is an ellipse. What, then, might an anti-inductivist, such as Popper, say about this example?

Popper, as we have seen, stresses that a considerable theoretical background is needed for making observations, and indeed there was a very significant theoretical background to Tycho Brahe's survey of the heavens. Copernicus' new theory of the universe had been published in 1543. By the 1570s there was a major theoretical dispute in astronomy between the upholders of the older Aristotelian–Ptolemaic view that the Earth was stationary at the centre of the universe and the Sun went round the Earth, and the Copernicans, who thought that the Sun was stationary at the centre and the Earth went round the Sun. Tycho Brahe's observations were relevant to this theoretical controversy. At a more basic level, even his division of heavenly bodies into stars and planets involved a theoretical classification. Indeed, this classification was different in the two contending theories. In the Ptolemaic theory, a planet was a heavenly body which was not a fixed star and which moved round the Earth; so the Sun was a planet, but the Earth was not a planet.

In the Copernican theory, a planet was a body which was not a fixed star and which moved round the Sun; so, on this account, the Sun was not a planet, but the Earth was.

Thus, Popper's approach is correct in that there was an important theoretical background to Tycho Brahe's observations. None the less, it remains true that Tycho Brahe's observations did precede Kepler's theorizing, and that part of the process which led Kepler to his laws was long and continuous study of the data which Tycho Brahe had collected. So some features of the inductivist account do apply here.

But this raises a problem. How do Tycho Brahe's valuable observations differ from the obviously valueless random observations which Popper parodies in his example of the man who wrote down everything he could observe and bequeathed his priceless collection of observations to the Royal Society to be used as inductive evidence? Part of the answer has already been given. Tycho Brahe's observations were made at a time when a controversy was raging between the Ptolemaic and the Copernican theories of the world, and his observations were clearly relevant to this controversy. Another point worth noting is that Tycho Brahe's observations were also relevant to a practical problem. Trade and shipping were developing rapidly at the time and brought with them the demand for better astronomical tables which could be used in navigation. It is significant that the King of Denmark, who financed Tycho Brahe's observatory, derived a large part of his royal income from tolls on ships passing through the Danish Sound, which connects the Baltic to the North Sea.

Kepler put his astronomical discoveries to practical use, employing them to compute a new set of astronomical tables. These were called the *Rudolfine Tables* after his patron King Rudolph II and were issued in 1627. They achieved new levels of accuracy, completely superseding all previous astronomical tables, and were at once used for navigational purposes.

So it does seem that it is worth collecting observations if these Baconian 'grapes . . . ripe and fully seasoned' are clearly relevant to a theoretical controversy or a practical application.

Let us turn now to another aspect of the problem. Kepler certainly arrived at his three laws by a process which involved a careful study of Tycho Brahe's data. Did he then infer his laws by some method like Baconian induction, and, if not, how did he obtain them? It will be convenient to examine these questions in connection with Kepler's discovery of his first law.

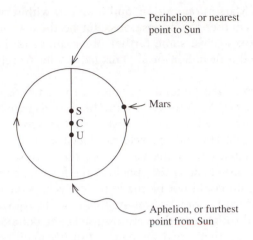

Fig. 1.1. Kepler's first hypothesis

How, then, did Kepler discover that the planet Mars moves in an ellipse with the Sun at one focus? The first point which needs to be stressed is that Kepler started his investigation with a number of theoretical assumptions. He was already a convinced Copernican and so related Mars's orbit to the Sun rather than the Earth. Indeed, he assumed that the Sun was a centre of force which governed the motions of the planets. If Kepler had tried to relate Mars to the Earth rather than to the Sun, he would never have found the elliptic orbit. He also began with the theoretical assumption that the motion of heavenly bodies was either circular or composed of a small number of circular motions. This assumption (which Kepler later rejected) had been made by astronomers since the time of Plato and Aristotle.

With these background assumptions, Kepler formulated his *first hypothesis*:

> The orbit of Mars is a circle round a centre C somewhat displaced from the sun S, and its motion is uniform with respect to a point U.

On this hypothesis (illustrated in Fig. 1.1) the planet moves faster when nearer the Sun, in conformity with the idea that the Sun is a centre of force influencing its motion.

Kepler made 900 folio pages in small handwriting of draft calculations relating to this hypothesis. He based it on four observed positions of Mars in opposition, and it agreed within two minutes of arc with another ten oppositions. But he then went on to test the hypothesis against some further observations of Tycho's, and this produced a deviation of 8′. This led Kepler to reject his first hypothesis.

Kepler next tried (second hypothesis) to compose the motion out of two circles. Mars moved round the second circle (or *epicycle*), whose centre moved round the first circle (or *deferent*). The combination of deferent and epicycle produced an egg-shaped curve with the pointed end at the perihelion, the nearest point to the Sun, and the broad end at the aphelion, the furthest point from the Sun. This again could not be made to fit Tycho's data.

Kepler's third hypothesis was mathematically equivalent to an ellipse, but, through a mathematical mistake, he got a curve which did not fit. He then tried an ellipse (fourth hypothesis) which worked, and subsequently realized that the third and fourth hypotheses were equivalent.

Now the striking thing about Kepler's work when we look at it in detail is how well it fits Popper's model of conjectures and refutations. Kepler produces a sequence of hypotheses which are each rejected until he finally hits on one which fits the data. Indeed Kepler appears to be a 'super-Popperian' when he rejects his very successful first hypothesis because of a deviation of only 8′. Popper, of course, particularly commends scientists who are prepared to abandon their hypotheses in the face of counter-evidence. Kepler knew that Tycho Brahe was a very careful and exact observer, and thought accordingly that Tycho Brahe's data could not contain errors as large as 8′. He therefore regarded the 8′ deviation as a refutation of his first hypothesis.

But how did Kepler come to formulate his successive hypotheses? It is out of the question that this was by any mechanical or Baconian process. Let us consider the crucial transition from hypothesis 2 to hypothesis 3. On the failure of hypothesis 2, Kepler could certainly have tried to obtain a more accurate fit by the use of further epicycles and equants. This had been the standard practice of astronomers for nearly 2,000 years. Instead he began to consider other geometrical curves, eventually coming up with the ellipse. Here surely is an example of one of those 'creative intuitions' or 'irrational elements' of which Popper speaks.

Thus Kepler's formulation of his successive hypotheses involved some kind of 'creative intuition', but, on the other hand, it also involved a careful study of Tycho Brahe's data. So it seems equally undeniable that some process of induction from observations was involved. As this process was not, however, mechanical or Baconian, I propose to call it *intuitive induction*.[5] Of course, the words 'intuitive' and 'intuition' are rather vague. I will use them to describe some human mental process which results in the discovery of something new, but whose character remains obscure and mysterious, even to the human involved. Thus intuitive thinking can be contrasted with thinking which is routine, mechanical, or rule-guided. Reasoning of the latter kind can be carried out by a computer following a program or by a human using pen and paper, but intuitive reasoning, as I will use the term, is something that is exclusively human. Of course it remains possible that human intuitive reasoning is really mechanical and rule-guided, and only appears strange and mysterious because the mechanical rule-following goes on without the subject's conscious awareness. It will not, however, be necessary, for the purposes of this book, to pursue the question of whether this is so or not.

This concludes the analysis of Kepler's discovery of the laws of planetary motion with honours somewhat divided between Popper and the inductivists. Kepler's work certainly shows a very Popperian sequence of conjectures and refutations, but Tycho Brahe's observations were made before Kepler's theorizing took place, and that is an inductivist feature of the example. Moreover, Kepler certainly arrived at his hypotheses at least in part through a study of Tycho Brahe's data. So some process of induction was involved, though this was undoubtedly human intuitive rather mechanical induction. To find something mechanical (if not exactly Baconian), we need to look at another example from the history of science. This is the discovery of the sulphonamide drugs which will be considered in the next section.

1.4. The Discovery of the Sulphonamide Drugs

The sulphonamide drugs were discovered in Germany as a by-product of the activities of the giant chemical company I. G. Farben.[6] The discovery was made by a team headed by Gerhard Domagk, who was born in 1895 and appointed at the early age of 32 as director of research in experimental pathology and bacteriology in the institute attached to the I. G. Farben works at Elberfeld. Domagk and his team had huge laboratories in which they routinely tested compounds produced by the firm's industrial chemists on thousands of infected animals to see if the compounds had any therapeutic value.

The I. G. Farben chemists Hoerlin, Dressel, and Kothe produced a rich red dye which was very effective with protein materials such as wool and silk. This was known as *Prontosil rubrum*. Domagk and his team then discovered that this same compound possessed the definite ability to cure mice infected with haemolytic streptococci. Domagk published this finding in 1935, but referred back to experiments carried out in 1932.

At first sight this discovery may seem to be the lucky outcome of a more or less random search. However, this appearance is misleading. Domagk and his team made very definite use of heuristic considerations. A *heuristic* (from the Greek *heuriskein* 'to discover') is a guide to discovery. The search procedure which led to the discovery of *Prontosil rubrum*, the first of the sulphonamide drugs, did in fact make use of various heuristics. One of these was the idea that dyes capable of staining textiles might also have useful therapeutic properties. The 'dye heuristic', as it might be called,[7] had been introduced before Domagk by one of his teachers: Paul Ehrlich. Ehrlich discovered that, if certain dyes are injected into living organisms, they are taken up and stain only some particular tissues and not others. Ehrlich gives the following example, which played an important role in his discovery of the method of 'vital staining':

Thus, for example, methylene blue causes a really wonderful staining of the peripheral nervous system.

If a small quantity of methylene blue is injected into a frog, and a small piece of the tongue is excised and examined, one sees the finest twigs of the nerves beautifully stained, a magnificent dark blue, against a colourless background. (Ehrlich 1906: 235)

Ehrlich goes on to observe that this specific staining property is lost if the chemical composition of the dye is changed even to a small extent. Thus, he says:

I was able to prove that the nerve-staining property of methylene blue is conditioned by the presence of sulphur in the methylene-blue molecule. Synthetic chemistry has, in fact, given us a dye which, apart from the absence of sulphur, corresponds exactly in its chemical constitution to methylene blue. This is BINDSCHEDLER's green. With the absence of the sulphur, there is associated the inability to stain living nerves. (Ehrlich 1906: 235)

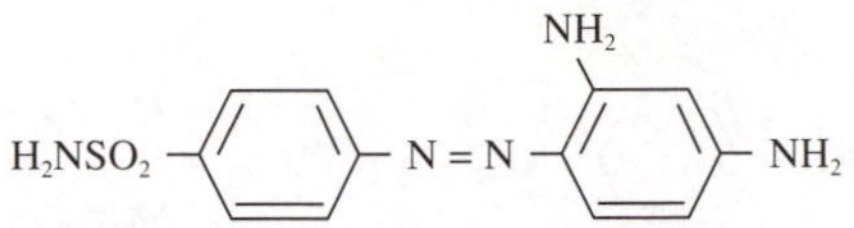

Fig. 1.2. The molecular structure of *Prontosil rubrum*

In the light of these interesting discoveries, Ehrlich reasoned somewhat as follows. Suppose we know that a particular disease is caused by the invasion of some micro-organisms. To cure the disease, we need to find a chemical which is highly toxic to these micro-organisms, but which does not harm the patient. This can be achieved if we can find a chemical which kills the micro-organisms *and* which is taken up only by the micro-organisms and not by the other tissues. Now dyes like methylene blue are highly specific, in that they are taken up by some tissues and not by others. Many dyes are also toxic. So it is not unreasonable to think that some dyes might have good therapeutic properties. Indeed, Ehrlich was able to show that his favourite, methylene blue, was helpful in curing malaria. As he says: 'In my further experiments . . . I started from the supposition that dyes with maximal tinctorial activity might also have a special affinity for parasites within the host-organism . . . I chose the malaria parasites and was able, in association with Professor GUTTMANN, to show that methylene blue can cure malaria' (Ehrlich 1906: 241).

So the 'dye heuristic' proved successful first for Ehrlich, then for Domagk. Ironically, however, it turned out that the therapeutic properties of *Prontosil rubrum* have nothing to do with its ability to dye fabrics.

The molecular structure of Prontosil rubrum is shown in Fig. 1.2, where the hexagons are benzene rings and, as usual, N denotes one atom of nitrogen, S of sulphur, O of oxygen, and H of hydrogen. It is clear that the molecule consists of two halves joined by the double bond denoted by =. In the human body, four hydrogen atoms are added to the molecule through the action of enzymes, and the molecule splits into two different molecules, sulphanilamide and tri-amino-benzene (see Fig. 1.3).

Now it turned out that only one of these molecules (sulphanilamide) is responsible for killing the pathogenic bacteria. Sulphanilamide, however, has no power of dyeing or staining either textiles or bacteria!

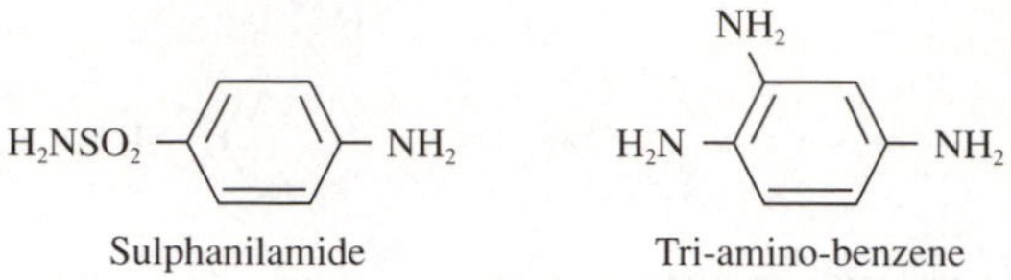

Sulphanilamide   Tri-amino-benzene

Fig. I.3. Reduction of *Prontosil rubrum* in the body

Sulphanilamide was the first of the sulphonamide drugs, and other drugs in the same group were discovered by experimenting with the effects of variants of the sulphanilamide molecule. That concludes my account of the discovery of the sulphonamide drugs, and I will next consider what light it sheds on the controversy between inductivism and falsificationism. As in the previous example, we have to conclude that honours are somewhat divided between the contending knights: Sir Francis and Sir Karl.

Let me begin with a point in favour of Popper. The sequence of events leading to the discovery of the first of the sulphonamide drugs can be described very nicely using the schema of conjectures and refutations. As each new compound was produced by I. G. Farben's industrial chemists, it was conjectured that it might have the ability to cure one or more bacterial infections. This conjecture was then tested by administering the compound to infected animals and seeing whether any improvement resulted. In the case of nearly all the compounds produced, the conjecture was refuted, but at last a compound appeared for which the corresponding conjecture was confirmed. In this case, however, the conjectures were not produced using human insight or creativity, but in a routine fashion. Thus the procedure could be called *mechanical falsificationism*.

Turning now to the views of the other contender, it is clear that the discovery of the sulphonamide drugs has many Baconian features. To begin with, Bacon stresses the desirability of teamwork in the sciences. Referring to his proposed method, he says:

it is not a way over which only one man can pass at a time (as is the case with that of reasoning), but one in which the labours and industries of men (especially as regards the collecting of experience), may with the best effect be first distributed and then combined. For then only will men begin to know their strength when instead of great numbers doing all the same things, one shall take charge of one thing and another of another. (Bacon 1620: 293)

Far from emphasizing insight, imagination, or creativity, Bacon seems to want to make science into a routine activity which could be carried out by anyone of average intelligence. As he says in a passage already quoted: 'But the course I propose for the discovery of sciences is such as leaves but little to the acuteness and strength of wits, but places all wits and understandings nearly on a level' (Bacon 1620: 270). Thus the army of scientists in Domagk's laboratories performing routine tests on routinely generated hypotheses seems to conform well to Bacon's ideas.

Bacon also had a very pragmatic attitude to the sciences. He considered that their aim was to improve technology (or 'the arts', as he described it in the language of his time). Moreover, he thought that technological improvements were of the greatest benefit to human beings. As he says:

the introduction of famous discoveries appears to hold by far the first place among human actions . . . For the benefits of discoveries may extend to the whole race of man . . . let a man only consider what a difference there is between the life of men in the most civilized province of Europe, and in the wildest and most barbarous districts of New India . . . And this difference comes not from soil, not from climate, not from race, but from the arts. (Bacon 1620: 300)

Bacon further predicted, quite correctly as it turned out, that the pursuit of science would lead to technological innovations of a character quite different from any that had hitherto appeared. 'There is therefore much ground for hoping that there are still laid up in the womb of nature many secrets of excellent use, having no affinity or parallelism with any thing that is now known, but lying entirely out of the beat of the imagination, which have not yet been found out' (1620: 292). Now the sulphonamide drugs were certainly a secret of excellent use.

Despite all these Baconian features, I do not think that the discovery of the sulphonamide drugs can correctly be described as an instance of Baconian or mechanical induction.[8] The process was undoubtedly *mechanical* to some extent, but it was not really *inductive*. Induction can best be defined as a procedure for obtaining laws, hypotheses, or perhaps predictions, from a mass of previously collected data.[9] Now each time I. G. Farben produced a new dye, a conjecture was routinely generated—namely, that the new dye might have therapeutic properties. This conjecture was not, however, obtained from any body of previously collected data, but from a heuristic principle, namely Ehrlich's 'supposition that dyes with maximum tinctorial activity might also have a special affinity for parasites within the host-organism'. Thus the discovery of the sulphonamide drugs seems to me correctly described as *mechanical falsificationism*, but *not* as *Baconian induction*.

The example of the discovery of the sulphonamide drugs has introduced the concept of *heuristics*, a concept which has the greatest importance for artificial intelligence. This then is an appropriate moment to make the transition from the present chapter, which deals with scientific method, to the next chapter, which introduces some material from artificial intelligence. Before doing so, it will be useful to make one last remark about heuristics, which will further help to link the two chapters. In the example of the discovery of the sulphonamide drugs, the heuristic principle used can be considered as part of the *background knowledge* (or *assumptions*) of the scientists working in the field. The dye heuristic, as we have seen, was a supposition of Ehrlich's which was, in effect, a generalization of some of the results which Ehrlich had obtained from his work on vital staining and on the cure of malaria. This principle that heuristics can be identified with background knowledge (or assumptions) seems to me to hold in a large number, perhaps even all, cases. In particular we shall see that machine-learning programs in the Turing tradition always include background knowledge in some coded form, and that this background knowledge guides the program in its search for a hypothesis which fits the data, thus acting as heuristic. For more details of this and related matters, let us now turn to Chapter 2.

2 Machine Learning in the Turing Tradition

In Chapter 1 we examined a long-standing controversy in the philosophy of science, that between *inductivism* (as represented principally by Bacon) and *falsificationism* (as represented principally by Popper). The method adopted for discussing this debate was also fairly traditional. We considered how well the two models of scientific method accounted for two examples from the history of science—namely, Kepler's discovery of the laws of planetary motion and the discovery of the sulphonamide drugs. These examples did not agree entirely with either Bacon or Popper. Kepler seems to have used some kind of inductive reasoning (in agreement with Bacon rather than Popper), but this was an *intuitive induction* involving human insight and creativity and so distinct from the kind of mechanical induction advocated by Bacon. By contrast, the discovery of the sulphonamide drugs was a much more mechanized process, but it seemed better described as *mechanical falsificationism* rather than as Baconian induction. The key point was that the hypotheses tested were generated mechanically from the heuristic (or background knowledge), and not from the observed data, as Baconian induction proper would require.

I think that a further examination of famous discoveries from the history of science would reveal a very similar picture, and that the method of mechanical induction as described and advocated by Bacon in his *Novum Organum* of 1620 has hitherto been applied very little, or not at all, in the development of science. This situation has, however, been changed by advances in a branch of artificial intelligence known as machine learning[1] made in the last twenty-five years or so. These developments are thus likely to bring about a profound change in the way that science is practised.

My aim then in Chapters 2 and 3 is to show how, as a result of developments in machine learning, something which can appropriately be described as *Baconian induction* may now be said to exist, and indeed to be in regular use. I will begin in this chapter (Chapter 2) by explaining some of the relevant recent results in machine learning, and by showing how they were developed. Then in the next chapter (Chapter 3) I will examine the importance of these results for the philosophy of science. Although the full discussion of the philosophical implications of machine learning is the task of the next chapter, it will be useful to give here a brief summary of some of the conclusions that will be reached there. The rationale for this proceeding is that it will throw into relief some important features of the machine-learning algorithms to be described later. These features are relevant to the philosophical conclusions I want to draw, but they might be overlooked if these conclusions are not kept in mind. The philosophical conclusions are in fact three in number, and I will consider them in turn.

The first conclusion is that machine-learning algorithms have brought into existence what could be called *inductive rules of inference* or (IRIs). An inductive rule of inference is a mechanical method for generating hypotheses from data. It is important to stress that such a rule should be *mechanical*—that is, it should not involve any human insight or creativity. Such rules lie at the heart of anything properly described as Baconian induction. However (and this will be the second conclusion), the actual rules which have been developed have a feature which Bacon himself did not consider or even suspect. They take the form: From K & e, derive H; *not* the form: From e alone, derive H, where, as usual, e is the evidence (or data), H is the hypothesis generated to explain e, and K is the background knowledge (or background assumptions/conjectures). In *mechanical falsificationism*, the (mechanical) rules of inference used are of the form: From K, derive H. These rules are thus *not inductive* rules of inference of the form: From K & e, derive H. This is where mechanical falsificationism differs from Baconian induction, in the full or proper sense. On the other hand (and this is the third conclusion), Baconian induction, like mechanical falsificationism, does involve a falsificationist component. As we shall see, the various machine-learning algorithms, or *general* inductive rules of inference (*general* IRIs), consist of a *basic* inductive rule of inference (*basic* IRI) which is then iterated to produce the final hypothesis. Testing and falsification always play a key role in this iteration process. So, while the advances in machine learning have, on the whole, supported

Bacon rather than Popper, the new inductive inferences do make an important use of Popperian procedures.

To sum up then. When we examine various machine-learning algorithms in the next few sections, attention will be drawn to the following three features:

1. the existence of inductive rules of inference (or IRIs);
2. the role of background knowledge (K), as well as data (e) in these rules;
3. the role of testing and falsification in the process of iterating a basic inductive rule of inference to produce the final result.

2.1. The Turing Tradition

It is certainly not the aim of this chapter to write a complete history of developments in machine learning in the last twenty-five years. That would be far too ambitious a project for our purposes, and maybe it is too early to attempt such a thing. Instead I will concentrate on only one strand of development, to which I propose giving the name *the Turing tradition*.[2] This tradition can be characterized either by the way it was handed on (like the apostolic succession) in a chain leading back to Turing himself; or by the fact that it embodies some principles and a methodology actually used by Turing. I will start with the second characterization, which is obviously the more important from the theoretical point of view.

The features which seem to me to characterize the Turing tradition are (i) the use of logic and (ii) close attention to practical problems; or, in short, logic and practice. What gives the tradition its peculiar flavour is this particular combination, for few logicians are interested in practical applications and few practical men or women have an interest in logic. We can see that logic and practice characterized Turing's own work by considering his most famous contribution—the Turing machine. Turing introduced his machine in his 1936–7 paper, which was concerned with a problem in abstract logical theory posed by Hilbert—the *Entscheidungsproblem*. However the concept of the Turing machine, which arose from these abstract considerations, had none the less quite a concrete character, and the theory of Turing machines was actually used by Turing in his later attempts to design a real working computer. (For details, see Hodges 1983: particularly ch. 6, pp. 318 ff.)

Machine Learning in the Turing Tradition

Logic here mainly comprises deductive logic, but the term should perhaps be extended to include probability. For his work in cracking the German enigma code, Turing used a probability-based measure of weight of evidence, which was later developed by his wartime assistant Good. (For details, see Gillies 1990.) Recently several of those developing machine learning in the Turing tradition have begun to make extensive use of probabilistic considerations (see e.g. Džeroski and Bratko 1992).

We can illustrate this emphasis on logic and practice within the Turing tradition by considering Ehud Shapiro's (1983) *Algorithmic Program Debugging*.[3] As the title suggests, this is concerned with the practical problem of debugging programs. In his approach to this problem, Shapiro makes extensive use of logic, and attributes to this the success he achieved. As he says: 'The second main result . . . is the development of a general, incremental inductive inference algorithm, that is simple enough to be analyzed theoretically, and is amenable to an implementation that compares favorably with other inductive inference systems. We attribute this success to the choice of logic as the target computational model' (Shapiro 1983: 158). In this respect, as in others, Shapiro is in the mainstream of the Turing tradition.

Since any approach can be better understood by contrasting it to another based on different principles, I will briefly compare the Turing tradition in machine learning to another which has, in my view, been distinctly less successful. This is the approach adopted by Herbert Simon and his co-workers (see Langley, Simon, Bradshaw, and Zytkow 1987). Simon and his group consider case studies of scientific discoveries made by human scientists, and then try to write computer programs to simulate these discoveries. Thus, for example, they have produced a computer program called BACON.1 which is described in Langley *et al.* (1987: 66–86). Among its other achievements, BACON.1 discovered Kepler's third law when given some of the data available to Kepler. As Simon himself says: 'Computer programs exist today that, given the same initial conditions that confronted certain human scientists, remake the discoveries the scientists made. BACON, described at length in Langley *et al.*, is one such program' (Simon 1992: 4).

The approach of Simon and his group can be described as *psychological* as opposed to the *logical* approach of those working in the Turing tradition. Simon and his group start by studying the inductive inferences made by some famous human scientist, and then try to simulate these by a computer program. Those working in the Turing tradition, by contrast, construct the basic inductive rules of inference which are at the heart of their algorithms by a process of logical analysis which has no reference to the way in which humans reason inductively. We shall examine some examples of this type of logical analysis later on.

It may now be asked why I take such a critical attitude to the work of Simon and his group. Their approach is based on a plausible idea, and they have succeeded in simulating the discoveries of famous scientists. Why, then, do I judge their work to be a failure? The answer is simple. Simon and his group have indeed 'rediscovered' (in some sense) laws already known. Their programs have not, however, discovered any new and important rules, generalizations, or laws. Moreover, the discovery of a new and significant generalization seems to me the crucial test of whether a machine-learning program has really been successful. The failure of Simon and his group in this respect is in sharp contrast to the remarkable successes of those working in the Turing tradition, some of which will be described later on. Machine learning in the Turing tradition has produced effective rules and generalizations in areas where none was previously known. In other areas, where some rules had already been obtained, the programs were able to generate new rules which performed more satisfactorily than those produced by humans. Simon and his group do not have any successes of this kind to their credit.

Granted, then, that the *logical* approach of the Turing tradition has proved more successful than the *psychological* approach of Simon and his group, it is interesting to enquire why this has been so. There seem to me to be three reasons. First of all let us consider an analogy with the problem of mechanical theorem-proving. A human mathematician, working informally, produces a proof in which it is immediately (or intuitively) obvious, at least to the skilled mathematician, that one line follows from the previous one. However, these 'self-evident' inferences are often in reality very complicated, involving perhaps a combination of several logical inferences and intuitive assumptions. Those who worked in the logicist and formalist programmes for the foundations of mathematics, notably Frege, Peano, and Russell, set themselves the task of replacing these informal proofs by fully formalized proofs in which each step would be justified by a simple logical inference. This is how Frege explains the project in a passage from his (1884) *Foundations of Arithmetic*. He writes:

the mathematician rests content if every transition to a fresh judgement is self-evidently correct, without enquiring into the nature of this self-evidence, whether it is logical or intuitive. A single such step is often really a whole compendium, equivalent to several simple inferences, and into it there can still creep along with these some element from intuition. In proofs as we know them, progress is by jumps, which is why the variety of types of inference in mathematics appears to be so excessively rich; for the bigger the jump, the more diverse are the combinations it can represent of simple inferences with axioms derived from intuition. Often, nevertheless, the correctness of such a transition is immediately self-evident to us, without our ever becoming conscious of the subordinate steps condensed within it; whereupon, since it does not obviously conform to any of the recognized types of logical inference, we are prepared to accept its self-evidence forthwith as intuitive . . .

The demand is not to be denied: every jump must be barred from our deductions. That it is so hard to satisfy must be set down to the tediousness of proceeding step by step. Every proof which is even a little complicated threatens to become inordinately long. And moreover, the excessive variety of logical forms that has gone into the shaping of our language makes it difficult to isolate a set of modes of inference which is both sufficient to cope with all cases and easy to take in at a glance.

To minimize these drawbacks, I invented my concept writing. It is designed to produce expressions which are shorter and easier to take in, and to be operated like a calculus by means of a small number of standard moves, so that no step is permitted which does not conform to the rules which are laid down once and for all. It is impossible, therefore, for any premiss to creep into a proof without being noticed. (Frege 1884: 102–3)

What is significant about this passage is that Frege refuses to be content with inferences just because they are 'immediately self-evident to us'. On the contrary, he makes the demand that 'every jump must be barred from our deductions' and that 'no step is permitted which does not conform to the rules which are laid down once and for all'. Formal logic as we know it today was born from the struggle to achieve these goals.[4]

We can now see that the work of formalizing proofs carried out by Frege, Peano, Russell, and so on was a necessary pre-condition for the implementation of mechanical theorem-provers. Such a theorem-prover has to use formal proofs based on clearly specified rules of deductive inference. For example, the theorem-prover used by PROLOG, which we will consider in Chapter 4, uses a single rule of inference: resolution. The formalization of humanly comprehensible informal proofs was thus clearly needed before a mechanical theorem-prover could be produced. Suppose someone working on mechanical theorem-proving had ignored the step of logical analysis and formalization of informal proofs and had followed a methodology similar to that of Simon and his group, taking informal proofs produced by great mathematicians such as Gauss and trying to simulate them on the computer. Such a procedure would have been very unlikely to meet with any success. A great mathematician such as Gauss would undoubtedly have proceeded by jumps involving (in Frege's words) 'combinations of simple inferences . . . with axioms derived from intuition', and it would have been well-nigh impossible to isolate from these an appropriate 'set of modes of inference'. The inductive case is very much the same. A great scientist such as Kepler would similarly use inductive jumps, from which it would be very difficult to isolate an appropriate set of simple modes of inference. The way to obtain such modes of inference is to follow the logical path of the Turing tradition—in other words, to obtain basic rules of inductive inference from the logical analysis of simple cases and then to obtain more complicated rules of inductive inference by the iteration of these basic ones. This is not to say, of course, that the study of important events in the history of science, such as the work of Kepler and Domagk, is of no value. On the contrary, much can be learnt from such case studies. They show, for example, the importance of heuristics/background knowledge and illustrate the role of testing and falsification. They are not, however, suitable for formulating computer-usable rules of inductive inference. This is, in my view, the fundamental reason for the lack of success of Simon and his group, but there are two further defects in their methodology which we must next consider.

Simon and his group concentrate on replicating the discovery of laws which are already known, but, just because the answer (the law) is already known, features of it may be built into the program which is designed to do the discovering. I have argued elsewhere[5] that this is in fact the case with the program BACON.1's discovery of Kepler's third law. The law states that $D^3/P^2 = $ constant for all planets, where D is the mean distance of the planet from the Sun, and P is its period. The program is given values for the variables D and P and told to relate them, but this is, in effect, giving it the result of one of Kepler's big innovations. D, the mean distance of the planet from the Sun, would have had no significance in the dominant paradigm of Ptolemaic astronomy. No normal scientist of the time would have considered it. Then again, the program is, in effect, told to look for a law of the form $x^m y^n = $ constant. Kepler did indeed search for a law of this form, but this was another of his remarkable innovations. Ellipses had been studied in antiquity, but a law of the form $x^3 y^{-2} = $ constant was a complete novelty.

The computer is, in effect, told (i) which two variables to relate and (ii) the general form of the law it should look for. The really difficult part of Kepler's discovery was finding out (i) and (ii), and this BACON.1 does not do at all. Once (i) and (ii) are given, the problem reduces to estimating two parameters from the data. BACON.1 does succeed in carrying out this step, but it is the easiest step, and, moreover, there is nothing surprising in a computer program estimating a few parameters in a given model. Taking logs we get $m \log D + n \log P = $ constant. So all we have to do is estimate from data the parameters m, n in the simple linear model $m x + n y = $ constant. This can be done by very familiar statistical techniques, and BACON.1 does no more than provide an alternative solution to this elementary problem. It is thus not surprising that it is not able to discover any new and significant generalizations.

The third problem with the methodology of Simon and his group is that they have not tried to apply their machine-learning techniques to any practical problem. Success in practice is, however, one of the key tests of the efficacy of any technique in artificial intelligence. If the technique provides a solution to a hitherto un-solved practical problem, or a new and improved solution where a perhaps not very satisfactory solution already existed, then there can be no question of the programmer having obtained an already known solution after computation by building in parts of it at the beginning before computation. The test of practice is thus very im-portant for artificial intelligence, and it is wise to be sceptical about anything in the field which does not pass this test.

So far I have characterized the Turing tradition theoretically in terms of its emphasis on logic and practice, and have contrasted it with the psychological approach of Simon and his group. The tra-dition can, however, also be characterized by tracing the flow of ideas from person to person back to Turing himself. The key figure here is Donald Michie, who worked with Turing at Bletchley on cryptanalysis during the war and then went on to found the De-partment of Artificial Intelligence at Edinburgh University and the Turing Institute in Glasgow. Donald Michie played a key role in disseminating the ideas of the Turing tradition and encouraging talented researchers to work in this line. It is striking how many key articles and books carry an acknowledgement to Donald Michie (e.g. Muggleton 1992; Quinlan 1979, 1986; Shapiro 1983, etc.). Thus Shapiro says: 'Donald Michie's enthusiasm about my research was an ultimate source of pleasure, and helped me feel that what I am doing may be worth while' (1983: p. ix), and Quinlan: 'It is a pleasure to acknowledge the stimulus and suggestions provided over many years by Donald Michie, who continues to play a central role in the development of this methodology' (1986: 104). Many of those involved in the Turing tradition spent some time with Michie either in Edinburgh or in Glasgow, but it is also interesting to note that the group is quite spread out geographically and has members from many nations, including Australia, Britain, Slovenia, the USA, and, more recently, Japan. This is a new development in the history of ideas, for, in the past, groups with a shared intellectual approach tended to be located at the same place. Now, however, with the greater ease of communication at a distance through the development of travel, regular conferences, and e-mail, it is possible for a group to share an approach and work interactively while being very dispersed geographically. The AI community is at the forefront of this new sociological pattern of research.

I have stressed the emphasis on practical applications in the Turing tradition, and it is therefore logical to begin my account of their work by describing the practical problem which set their research in motion. This has the rather exotic name of 'Feigenbaum's bottleneck', and will be considered in the next section.

2.2. The Practical Problem: Expert Systems and Feigenbaum's Bottleneck

The first major practical success of artificial intelligence was the development and application of expert systems, and this in turn gave rise to 'Feigenbaum's bottleneck'. I will begin, therefore, with a brief sketch of the nature of expert systems and their early history, and this will lead us naturally to the bottleneck in question.[6]

An expert system is a computer program designed to perform the task normally performed by an expert. An obvious example is medical diagnosis. The computer would be fed with data about the patient, including perhaps the results of tests performed on the patient, and would then output a diagnosis of the illness from which the patient is suffering. The characteristic feature of expert systems

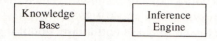

Fig. 2.1. The two parts of an expert system

is that they use a symbolic representation of the knowledge employed by a human expert. Hence the term 'knowledge-based systems'. An expert system then consists of two parts: (*a*) a knowledge base and (*b*) an inference engine (see Fig. 2.1). If presented with a query, the computer will try to infer the answer from the knowledge base, using the logic and heuristics in the inference engine.

The creation of the knowledge base poses a number of problems. One of these arises from the fact that the knowledge must be represented in a symbolic form in which it can be stored and used by the computer. This is known as the *knowledge representation problem*. There have been a number of suggestions as to how knowledge might be represented, but the most popular and successful is as a set of rules. Hence the term 'rule-based systems'. In the medical case, a simple rule might be: 'If the patient coughs blood, then probably he or she has a lung disease.' If this rule is in the knowledge base, and the computer is fed the datum 'Mr A coughs blood', its inference engine should enable it to infer: 'Mr A probably has a lung disease.'

Expert systems were invented by the Stanford Heuristic Programming project. The first such system is known as DENDRAL. It was developed by Edward Feigenbaum, Bruce Buchanan, and others from 1965 onwards, in collaboration with the Stanford Mass Spectrometry Laboratory. In a mass spectrometer, an organic compound is bombarded with high-energy particles, causing pieces of the molecule to break away. The masses and relative abundance of these fragments are recorded, and this is called the mass spectrogram of the compound. The problem is to infer a plausible molecular structure for the compound from its atomic composition and mass spectrogram. This is no easy matter and in 1965 required the skills of an expert chemist. DENDRAL was designed to offer computer assistance in the process, a goal which it accomplished successfully. For further details about the system, see Buchanan and Feigenbaum (1978).

The first medical expert system MYCIN was also developed by the Stanford Heuristic Programming Project. Work on the system was started by Edward Shortliffe and others in 1975 in collaboration with the Infectious Diseases group at the Stanford Medical School. The program diagnoses blood and meningitis infections and recommends appropriate drug treatment. Its knowledge base comprises over 400 rules. Here is an example:

Rule 85

IF:

    (1) The site of the culture is blood, and
    (2) The gram stain of the organism is gramneg, and
    (3) The morphology of the organism is rod, and
    (4) The patient is a compromised host

THEN:

There is suggestive evidence (0.6) that the identity of the organism is pseudo-aeruginosa.

Further details about MYCIN are to be found in Davis, Buchanan, and Shortliffe (1977).

There is always some doubt about just how well expert systems work, and, in an attempt to resolve this, MYCIN along with nine human doctors sat an examination in 1979. The program's final conclusions on ten real cases were compared with those of the human doctors, including the actual therapy administered. Eight other experts were then asked to rate the ten therapy recommendations and award a mark, without knowing which, if any, came from a computer. They were requested to give 1 for a therapy which they regarded as acceptable and 0 for an unacceptable therapy. Since there were eight experts and ten cases, the maximum possible mark was 80. The results were as follows (taken from Jackson 1986: 106):

MYCIN	52	Actual therapy	46
Faculty-1	50	Faculty-4	44
Faculty-2	48	Resident	36
Inf dis fellow	48	Faculty-5	34
Faculty-3	46	Student	24

So MYCIN came first in the exam, though the difference between it and the top human experts was not significant.

By the end of the 1970s it had become clear that expert systems were a practically useful AI technique, and computer scientists began to build such systems for a whole variety of applications. One of the main difficulties in so doing was eliciting the knowledge required for the rule base from the human domain experts. These experts certainly knew how to perform the task, but they often found it very difficult to state explicitly the knowledge required to do so. The procedure used for constructing the first expert systems such as DENDRAL and MYCIN consisted in the computer scientists conducting long interviews with the domain experts in the attempt to formulate the required rules, but the results often contained omissions and inconsistencies which had to be laboriously tracked down and rectified. Concerning this, Quinlan observes: 'While the typical rate of knowledge elucidation by this method is a few rules per man day, an expert system for a complex task may require hundreds or even thousands of such rules. It is obvious that the interview approach cannot keep pace with the burgeoning demand for expert systems . . .' (1986: 82). Feigenbaum wrote in 1977: 'the acquisition of domain knowledge [is] the bottleneck problem in the building of applications-oriented intelligent agents.'[7] So the problem has become known as Feigenbaum's bottleneck.

Actually the difficulty is not just a matter of the time it takes to elicit knowledge from domain experts by the interview method. In some cases the experts may simply not know how they perform their skilled task, even though they perform it very well. In such cases interviews will have no success in producing a knowledge base for the computer to use. Michie has an amusing apocryphal story which illustrates the point very nicely. He writes:

Unfortunately, human practitioners tend to describe their own rules of operation in terms which do not subsequently stand the test of practice. The story is told of a large cheese factory whose camemberts were a byword. Crucial to their renown was the company's procedure for quality control, by which every hundredth cheese was sampled to ensure that the production process was still on the narrow path separating the marginally unripe from the marginally over-ripe. Success rested on the uncanny powers developed by one very old man, whose procedure was to thrust his index finger into the cheese, close his eyes, and utter an opinion.

If only because of the expert's age and frailty, automation seemed to be required, and an ambitious R&D project was launched. After much escalation of cost and elaboration of method, which included lowering into the cheeses various steel probes wired to strain gauges and other sensors, no progress had been registered. Substantial inducements were offered to the sage for a precise account of how he did the trick. He could offer little, beyond the advice: 'It's got to *feel* right!' In the end it turned out that feel had nothing to do with it. After breaking the crust with his finger, the expert was interpreting subliminal signals from his sense of smell. (Michie 1982: 217)

As we shall see later, Michie's apocryphal story is very similar to something which actually occurred at the Jesenice Steel Mill in Slovenia.

Machine learning offers a possible solution to these difficulties. Instead of attempting painfully to extract the rules needed for the knowledge base from domain experts, the alternative strategy would be to try to induce the rules from examples using machine-learning techniques. This was the practical goal of research into machine learning in the Turing tradition, and we shall see in Section 2.5 what success this research has had in achieving its goal.

It is important to stress, however, that the use of machine-learning techniques should not eliminate completely interviews with domain experts. Such experts may not easily be able to provide fully fledged rules, but they may be able without much difficulty to provide some background knowledge which is likely to be of use in obtaining the rules by machine-learning techniques. This point is made by Quinlan as follows:

Part of the bottleneck is perhaps due to the fact that the expert is called upon to perform tasks that he does not ordinarily do, such as setting down a comprehensive roadmap of some subject. (How often, for instance, is a mathematician asked to write down everything he knows about integration?) The expert may be adept at identifying landmarks, key concepts and so forth . . . The lure of induction techniques is the possibility of providing the expert with assistance where he needs it most. The expert will still be responsible for concepts or new ways of viewing objects in the domain and rules of thumb for navigating it. The synthesis of a complete, consistent explanation of the domain in terms of these concepts will then be handed over to an induction-based algorithm. (1979: 168)

The domain expert might also be able to provide convenient sets of examples which the machine-learning algorithm could then use to induce the requisite rules.[8]

Feigenbaum formulated his bottleneck problem in 1977, and the next few years saw the first attempts to develop machine-learning techniques for solving it. One of the first systems, Meta-DENDRAL, was designed to induce rules for use by DENDRAL. It succeeded in this task, and some of the rules were even published in a chemistry journal. Some details about the system are to be found in Buchanan and Feigenbaum (1978). At about the same time, Michalski produced a machine-learning system INDUCE, which was used by him and Chilautsky to obtain rules for an expert system concerned with the diagnosis of soybean disease. The rules were inferred from several hundred correctly diagnosed examples and were then compared with rules obtained from the domain experts. Michalski and Chilautsky attempted the inductive derivation of the rules, because the acquisition of rules through interviewing experts had proved to be so difficult and time-consuming. Thus they initially thought of the inductive approach as a 'short cut' and expected that it would not give such good results as the full interview approach. They were thus surprised to discover that the opposite was the case. As they say:

The inductive method presented in the paper required less effort and produced decision rules whose overall performance was somewhat better than expert derived rules. The latter result was contrary to the expectations of the authors, and therefore the experiment was repeated several times, introducing modifications to expert derived rules and trying different evaluation schemes. The results have consistently followed the same pattern. (Michalski and Chilautsky 1980: 150)

Michalski and Chilautsky go on to give an interesting analysis of why expert derived rules perform worse than inductively derived rules. On this point, they write:

A reason for the somewhat poorer performance of expert derived rules may be the insufficiently precise encoding of the decision rules of experts. It is likely that further interaction with experts and a refinement of the knowledge representation method will lead to better rules. Another possible reason is that experts are trained in making diagnoses, and not in explaining the process of diagnosis. These two functions are different. This would mean that examples of expert decisions represent more reliable information than experts' descriptions of the diagnostic procedures. This would provide an additional argument for the inductive method of knowledge acquisition. (Michalski and Chilautsky 1980: 150)

Another interesting finding of Michalski and Chilautsky was that the experts on the whole reacted favourably to the inductively derived rules. As they say: 'Surprisingly, the inductively derived rules were viewed generally quite favorably by experts—with a few exceptions. This observation and previous remarks suggest that a procedure in which an expert would edit inductively derived rules, in combination with an improved inductive program, could lead to an attractive new method of knowledge acquisition' (Michalski and Chilautsky 1980: 151).

A full history of machine learning would certainly have to lay great stress on such pioneering efforts as Meta-DENDRAL and the work of Michalski and Chilautsky. However, as already stressed, my intention is not to write a full history of machine learning, but rather to present some significant results in the Turing tradition, which have important implications for the controversy between inductivism and falsificationism. Accordingly I will examine only two machine-learning programs in detail. These are Quinlan's ID3 (Quinlan 1979, 1986) and Muggleton and Feng's GOLEM (Muggleton and Feng 1992). These examples are chosen, partly because they were very successful, but also because they illustrate many features of machine learning within the Turing tradition. The machine-learning methods developed fall into two broad classes: attribute-based learning and relational learning, while the algorithms used for the learning can be either top down or bottom up. ID3 is top down, and attribute based, while GOLEM is bottom up and relational, so that between them they gave a good idea of the range of techniques available. I will describe the workings of ID3 in the next section (2.3) and of GOLEM in the following section (2.4). Some of the successes of these (and closely related systems) will then be considered in Sections 2.5 and 2.6.

2.3. Attribute-Based Learning, Decision Trees, and Quinlan's ID3

Attribute-based learning is essentially concerned with classifying objects on the basis of sets of attributes. Let us take as an example the problem of classifying birds into swans and non-swans. We shall assume as an approximate simplification that this can be done using the attributes size, neck length, aquatic, and colour. We shall further assume that size has five values—namely, very large, large, medium, small, very small; that neck length has three values— namely, long, medium, short; that aquatic has two values—namely, true and false; and that colour has a very large, but finite, number of values, e.g. white, black, pink, . . . The aim is to find a law which correctly classifies birds into swans and non-swans. In our approximate simplification, the law might be:

> x is a swan if and only if x has size: large, x has neck length: long, x is aquatic, and x is white, or x has size: large, x has neck length: long, x is aquatic, and x is black.

In machine-learning terms, the problem could be formulated as follows. We are given a sample of birds, known as the *training set*.

Each member of the training set is fully described in terms of the set of attributes, and we are told which members of the set are swans and which are not swans. Those which are swans are called *positive instances* of the concept, and those which are not swans are called *negative instances* of the concept. The problem is to induce mechanically a correct classification law for swans which uses the given attributes. The law might be rather like the one just given.

It is clear that attribute-based learning is only a particular case of inductive learning. In logical terms, it has close affinities with the use of Aristotelian logic and propositional calculus. Aristotelian logic uses only 1-place predicates, such as 'x is mortal'. Now attributes are essentially equivalent to 1-place predicates. Some, such as 'x is aquatic', are indeed 1-place predicates, but even attributes which take several values can always be replaced by 1-place predicates. For example, the three-valued attribute neck length could be re-placed by the three 1-place predicates 'x has a long neck', 'x has a medium-length neck', and 'x has a short neck'. This then is the connection between attribute-based learning and Aristotelian logic. It is interesting here to note that Aristotle himself was particularly interested in biology and classification problems.

The connection between propositional calculus and attribute-based learning is equally clear. In the propositional calculus, compound propositions are built up from elementary propositions, using the connectives: and (&), or (v), not (¬), implies (→), . . . In attribute-based learning, the classification laws are built up from the attributes, by combining attributes using these same connectives. In the swan example, the attributes were combined using the connectives: and (&), or (v).

In modern logic, the first-order predicate calculus goes beyond both Aristotelian logic and propositional calculus in quite a number of ways. One of these is that it uses not just 1-place predicates, such as 'x is mortal', but 2-place predicates, such as 'x is to the left of y', 3-place predicates such as 'y is between x and z', and indeed n-place predicates for any finite n. Now n-place predicates with n > 1 are usually called *relations*. Thus any inductive learning problem which essentially involves the use of relations will go beyond the framework of attribute-based learning, and more of the resources of first-order predicate calculus will have to be introduced. This is what happens in relational learning, which we shall consider in the next section.

The fact that attribute-based learning uses a simple framework which is not adequate for many problems should not be taken as a criticism of the procedure. The framework, though simple, is in fact adequate for a wide range of practical problems, and for such problems it would be cumbersome to use a more complicated method. In general, a simpler method is to be preferred, provided that it is adequate for the problem in hand.

There are several machine-learning algorithms for attribute-based learning, but I will confine myself to describing one of the most famous and successful: Quinlan's ID3. This was developed from an earlier algorithm CLS (concept learning system), which had been devised by Earl Hunt and his collaborators and is described in Hunt, Marin, and Stone (1966). This development is interesting in terms of our characterization of the Turing tradition as involving logic combined with practice. The work of Hunt *et al.* certainly involves logical analysis, since they introduced algorithms, which were designed to learn laws formed from basic attributes by the using of the logical connectives. Just over a decade later, Quinlan was wrestling with the practical problem posed by Feigenbaum's bottle-neck, and he built on the work of Hunt *et al.* to produce machine-learning algorithms which did actually induce sets of rules needed for expert systems.

Quinlan's ID3, as an attribute-based learning system, is concerned to induce classification rules. Suppose, therefore, we have a set of instances which are each described in terms of a number of attributes. We want to develop a rule which classifies these instances into P (positive) or N (negative) on the basis of the attributes. It is assumed that it can be recognized in an individual case whether the instance is P or N, and the problem is to find, by mechanical induction from a training set, a rule which agrees with these individual judgements. The use of *positive* and *negative instances* of a concept in machine learning was introduced by Hunt *et al.* (see Hunt, Marin, and Stone 1966). Although it may seem an obvious procedure, it is in fact of considerable importance, and was first suggested by Bacon, as we shall see in the next chapter.

Quinlan (1986) gives the following simple example to illustrate these general ideas. The instances are Saturday mornings, and they are described by some weather attributes such as outlook, temperature, humidity, and so on. The aim here is to find a rule which classifies Saturday mornings into P (suitable for some unspecified activity), or N (unsuitable). In ID3, rules are given in the form of decision trees, of which Fig. 2.2 is a simple example. Note that

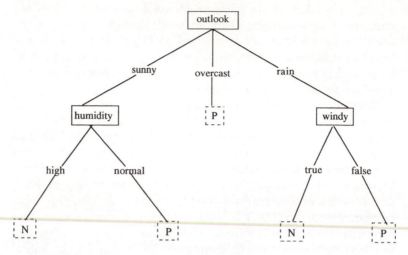

Fig. 2.2. A simple decision tree
Source: Quinlan (1986: 87)

decision trees, like most trees used by computer scientists, have the peculiarity that they grow downwards from their root to their leaves. Quinlan describes the way such a decision tree is used for classification as follows: 'In order to classify an object, we start at the root of the tree, evaluate the test, and take the branch appropriate to the outcome. The process continues until a leaf is encountered, at which time the object is asserted to belong to the class named by the leaf' (Quinlan 1986: 86–7). Thus if a particular Saturday morning has a sunny outlook with normal humidity, we classify it, according to the above decision tree, as P, i.e. suitable for the activity in question. The use of decision trees in machine learning was also introduced by Hunt, Marin, and Stone (1966), and it has proved extremely fruitful. In an earlier paper (1979) Quinlan makes an interesting comment on another simple example of a decision tree, and this perhaps helps to explain why the use of decision trees has been so successful.

Quinlan in fact introduced ID3 in his 1979 paper, and is concerned there with chess endings in which a white king and a white rook are opposed by a black king and a black knight. A chess-ending position of this kind with black to move can be classified into 'lost two ply' or 'not lost two ply'. The induction problem is to obtain a classification rule from a training set consisting of positive and

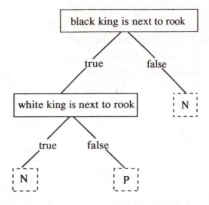

Fig. 2.3. Decision tree for 'the black king can take the white rook on its next move'

Source: Quinlan (1979: 173)

negative instances of this concept. Of course, this is a very complicated problem, but to illustrate the concept of decision tree, Quinlan considers the simpler concept 'the black king can take the white rook on its next move'. This can be defined by the decision tree given in Fig. 2.3. Quinlan now comments:

This rule is clearly isomorphic to the program fragment

 if *black king is next to rook*
 then if *white king is next to rook*
  then *cannot*
  else *can*
 else *cannot*

and it is just as easy to produce one as the other. The earlier form (called a *decision tree*) will be used for the rest of this article because it is somewhat more compact and easier to follow, but this should not obscure the relationship of inductive rule discovery to automatic programming. (Quinlan 1979: 173)

Perhaps, as Quinlan seems to suggest here, one of the reasons why it has proved fruitful to try to induce mechanically laws in the form of decision trees is that decision trees are similar to program fragments.

 Quinlan's ID3 has an algorithm for constructing a decision tree from some given data. His machine-learning program then proceeds by iteration of this algorithm. Let us begin by looking at the basic procedure.

We can construct a decision tree by choosing any of the attributes as a root. However, not all choices of attribute will be equally good. Some might result in small simple trees, and others in large complicated trees. In the original CLS of Hunt, Marin, and Stone (1966), the choice was made on a cost basis. At each stage, CLS explored the space of possible decision trees to a fixed depth, chose an action to minimize cost in this limited space, and moved one level down in the tree. ID3 abandons the cost-driven lookahead of CLS and uses instead an information-driven evaluation function. That attribute is chosen to branch on which gains the most information according to this evaluation function. The basic procedure now goes as follows. An attribute is chosen for the root of the tree by the information-gain criterion. If each value of this attribute corresponds to all positive or all negative instances—i.e. to a leaf of the tree—then we are done. If not, then at each value which has both positive and negative instances a new attribute is chosen by the information-gain criterion, and the tree is extended. This continues until the data are all divided into positive and negative instances—i.e. each branch of the tree terminates in a leaf. Of course, variants of ID3 can be produced by using criteria other than information gain for choosing the attribute on which to branch.

Let us now try to analyse this procedure in terms of inductive rules of inference (IRIs) and the use of testing and falsification to iterate a basic rule of inference. It is clear that the basic procedure in ID3 is easily and conveniently described in these terms. The basic IRI consists of filling an incomplete level in a decision tree (say the nth) by choosing attributes using the criterion of maximizing information gain. The result of this application of the basic IRI can be considered as the hypothesis that the resulting decision tree is a correct classification rule—i.e. that each branch will consist either of all positive instances or of all negative instances. This hypothesis is then tested out against the data, and, if a branch is discovered where there are both positive and negative instances, the hypothesis is regarded as falsified. The basic IRI is then applied again to fill in the incomplete n + 1th level, and so on until a correct decision tree is produced. Note that the data have to be used to calculate the information gain of the various attributes, and so to choose the next attribute for continuing the tree. This means that the basic IRI is indeed an IRI (inductive rule of inference) in the sense defined earlier—i.e. the hypothesis constructed depends on the data under consideration, or $H = f(e)$.

Another point to note is that the procedure is *top down* rather than *bottom up*. We can illustrate this distinction by considering two ways in which a classification rule for swans might be inferred inductively. Let us consider first Mr A, who makes inductive inferences in a top-down fashion. On observing one white swan on the River Thames near London, Mr A instantly proposes the generalization that all swans are white. However, he suspects that this generalization may be too sweeping, and he therefore tests it out by examining swans in other regions. First he looks at swans on other parts of the Thames, and finds them still white. Then he looks at swans on other rivers and lakes in England; still white. Then at swans in France, Italy, Germany, and so on; still white. Then he sails to Australia, and here the discovery of a black swan falsifies his original generalization. He therefore replaces it by something like: all European swans are white, and all Australian swans are black. Let us now contrast this with the procedure of Ms B, who makes inductive inferences in bottom-up fashion. On observing one white swan on the River Thames near London, she infers that all swans on the Thames near London are white. On examining swans on other parts of the Thames, she infers that all swans on the Thames are white. After looking at swans on other rivers and lakes in England, she infers that all English swans are white. Investigation of swans in France, Italy, Germany, and so on yields the conclusion that all European swans are white. Then she sails to Australia, and like Mr A ends up with the generalization that all European swans are white, and all Australian swans are black. In general then, top-down procedures start with simple and very general rules which are refuted and modified to produce more specific generalizations; while bottom-up procedures start with cautious, rather than sweeping, generalizations, and these are gradually extended in the light of further evidence. Popper always advocates making bold, sweeping, generalizations, and this corresponds to using a top-down procedure. However, as we shall see, bottom-up procedures have also been successful.

The basic procedure of ID3 is clearly top down. The first-level decision tree corresponds to the hypothesis that the single attribute chosen for the root is sufficient for classifying all objects into positive and negative instances. This is simple and general, and will usually be false. The discovery of counter-examples leads to the construction of ever more complicated and specific decision trees. In the next section, we shall see that GOLEM is, by contrast, a bottom-up procedure. Because of ID3's top-down nature, Quinlan refers to it and related machine-learning programs as the TDIDT (Top-Down Induction of Decision Trees) family.

We have so far described what has been called the *basic procedure* of ID3. The full ID3 program proceeds by iterating this basic procedure in a fashion which Quinlan describes as follows:

> The basic structure of ID3 is iterative. A subset of the training set called the *window* is chosen at random and a decision tree formed from it; this tree correctly classifies all objects in the window. All other objects in the training set are then classified using the tree. If the tree gives the correct answer for all these objects then it is correct for the entire training set and the process terminates. If not, a selection of the incorrectly classified objects is added to the window and the process continues. In this way, correct decision trees have been found after only a few iterations for training sets of up to thirty thousand objects described in terms of up to 50 attributes. (Quinlan 1986: 88)

The concept of *window* used here was introduced by Quinlan, who found that a correct decision tree is usually found more quickly by this iterative method than by forming a tree directly from the entire training set. ID3 thus involves a double iteration. In the first stage, the basic procedure is itself formed by iterating a basic inductive rule of inference. In the second stage, the basic procedure is treated as a basic inductive rule of inference (IRI) and iterated in the usual fashion. It is used to generate a hypothesis (decision tree) from the members of the window. This is then tested out against the training set as a whole, and, if it is falsified, a set of the counter-examples (falsifications) is added to the window, and the procedure is repeated. Popper's scheme of conjectures and refutations works well here, with the crucial difference that the conjectures are produced mechanically from part of the data.

This concludes my account of the main features of ID3. However, there is a further refinement of the procedure which is worth mentioning, since it deals with a problem which needs to be solved in order to produce any practical machine-learning system. So far we have assumed that any item of data which contradicts a suggested hypothesis should be regarded as a falsifying instance and lead to a modification of the hypothesis. In practice, however, most sets of data are imperfect and contain incorrect data points or 'noise'. There is thus a danger of producing unnecessarily complicated hypotheses by 'fitting the noise'. Quinlan modified ID3 by a statistical technique in order to deal with this problem. As he says:

An alternative method based on the chi-square test for stochastic independence has been found more useful. . . . The tree-building procedure can . . . be modified to prevent testing any attribute whose irrelevance cannot be rejected with a very high (e.g. 99%) confidence level. This has been found effective in preventing over-complex trees that attempt to 'fit the noise' without affecting performance of the procedure in the noise-free case. (Quinlan 1986: 93–4)

Quinlan then performed an interesting series of tests to see how well this procedure coped with noise. The method was to introduce noise by deliberating changing some correct data points to incorrect ones. A noise level of n per cent applied to a value meant that, with probability n per cent, the true value was replaced by a value chosen at random from among the values that could have appeared. Quinlan describes the results of these tests as follows:

low levels of noise do not cause the tree-building machinery to fall over a cliff. For this task, a 5% noise level in a single attribute produces a degradation in performance of less that 2%; a 5% noise level in all attributes together produces a 12% degradation in classification performance; while a similar noise level in class information results in a 3% degradation. Comparable figures have been obtained for other induction tasks. (Quinlan 1986: 94–5)

I have still not raised the question of background knowledge/assumptions in connection with ID3. My general thesis is that inductive rules of inference (IRIs) do not generate hypotheses from data alone (H = f(e)), but from data together with some background knowledge (or assumptions) K (H = f(K,e)). Now, is there some background knowledge involved in the IRIs of ID3, and, if so, what is its character? In generating its hypotheses (decision trees), ID3 selects at each stage an attribute from a set of attributes *which is given in advance*. The background assumption, which is a substantial one, is that this set of attributes is appropriate for describing the domain in question. If the attributes were inappropriate for describing the domain, then it would not be possible to generate satisfactory hypotheses. This is illustrated by considering again the example of Kepler's third law: $D^3/P^2 = c$ (constant). Here D is the mean distance of the planet from the Sun, while P is the planet's period. Now the point to note is that a normal scientist of Kepler's day would have been working in the Ptolemaic paradigm, and would therefore never have considered the parameter D; instead he would have considered D', the distance of the planet from the Earth.

However, with the choice of D′ instead of D, Kepler's elegant third law would never have been found. Kepler only obtained his third law, because, unusually for his time, he was a Copernican, and obviously, from the Copernican point of view, D rather than D′ was the key parameter to consider. This shows that the choice of basic attributes or parameters can be crucial for making successful inductive inferences, and, moreover, that this choice may depend upon rather deep theoretical assumptions.

We saw earlier that ID3 was developed from the system CLS devised by Hunt and his collaborators. Hunt *et al.* strongly emphasize the point that CLS generates new concepts only from given concepts. As they put it:

One must have a concept in order to learn more concepts. . . . when we speak of concept learning devices we are talking about devices which discover rules for combining previously learned concepts to form a new decision rule. At some point we must assume that the concept learner has some previously learned concepts, since these are needed to establish the description space. We shall have nothing at all to say about how these primitive constructs might be formed, by either a machine or a human being. (Hunt, Marin, and Stone 1966: 13)

Thus the set of previously learned concepts constitutes the background knowledge on which CLS operates.

Quinlan, in his 1982 paper 'Semi-Autonomous Acquisition of Pattern-Based Knowledge', makes some interesting points which again indicate the non-trivial nature of the assumption that the objects of a domain are to be described in terms of a particular set of attributes. As he says:

If two positions of different classes have the same attribute values, it is not possible for a decision tree that uses only these values to differentiate between them. In such a situation the attributes are termed *inadequate*, and the remedy is to define some further attribute capable of distinguishing between the troublesome positions.

Finding small but adequate sets of attributes for the king–rook king–knight problems was a considerable task (at least for a chess novice like the author)—hence the 'semi-autonomous' in this paper's title. (Quinlan 1982: 201)

Quinlan's term 'semi-autonomous' is very appropriate. It indicates that machine-learning programs do not generate hypotheses simply from data, but have to make use of background knowledge supplied by human investigators. Thus the computer is not fully

autonomous of human beings. This is a point of considerable philosophical importance to which we shall return later on.

2.4. GOLEM as an Example of Relational Learning

Quinlan's ID3 has had very considerable successes in a wide range
of applications. Quinlan himself (1986: 85) mentions the use of a
derivative of ID3 by Westinghouse Electric's Water Reactor Division in a fuel-enrichment application. This boosted the company's
revenue by more than ten million dollars per annum. We will give
further examples of successful applications of machine-learning
systems related to ID3 in Section 2.5 below.

Despite these successes, however, there are, as already pointed
out, limitations inherent in the TDIDT (Top-Down Induction of
Decision Trees) method. The approach deals only with objects described by a set of 1-place predicates, and induces only classification
rules of the decision-tree form. Now in many applications, the data
are described using more of the rich resources of the 1st-order
predicate calculus, and similarly it is often desirable to induce rules
which are formulated in 1st-order predicate calculus terms which
go beyond those involved in decision trees. Some recent research
has therefore focused on developing machine-learning programs
within the broader framework of 1st-order predicate calculus. For
the reasons explained above, this is known as *relational learning*.

Quinlan has been one of the pioneers in this area as well. In
Quinlan (1990), he presents a relational-learning system called FOIL,
which has been successful in a variety of applications. Although
FOIL differs from ID3 in being relational rather than attribute based,
it is similar to ID3 in being top down. So, in order to illustrate the
variety of machine-learning techniques, I will describe, not FOIL,
but another recent and successful relational-learning system called
GOLEM, which is bottom up rather than top down. This was developed by Muggleton and Feng (1992).

Both FOIL and GOLEM use the clausal form of 1st-order predicate calculus. This is the basis of the logic programming language
PROLOG, which will be described in Chapter 4. The clausal form
has shown itself via PROLOG to be an appropriate form of logic
for use in computing, and so is a natural choice for the development of relational-learning systems. For reasons of efficiency,
GOLEM is actually implemented in C, but it can conveniently be

thought of as being written in PROLOG. The C program is an efficient simulation of what is conceptually a PROLOG program. This accords with some methodological remarks of Shapiro, who defends PROLOG more as a method of thought than a practical programming system. He writes: 'the issue is the method of thought. Based on my experience . . . I maintain that one's thoughts are better organized, and one's solutions are clearer and more concise, if one thinks in Prolog . . .' (Shapiro 1983: 163). This is one aspect of the Turing tradition's emphasis on logical analysis as the basis of machine learning.

Just as ID3 was developed from earlier work by Hunt *et al.*, so GOLEM was developed from earlier work by Plotkin (1970, 1971*a*, *b*) carried out for his Ph.D. thesis at Edinburgh University. Plotkin's work, in turn, made use of results in Robinson (1965). Robinson (1965) introduced a form of logic suitable for theorem-proving on the computer. This is the clausal form of logic, which uses a single rule of inference: *the resolution principle*. As we shall see later (Sect. 4.1), Robinson's work was of crucial importance for the development of the logic programming system PROLOG. It also inspired Plotkin's work. Plotkin carried out his investigations in the clausal form of logic, and also made use of the concept of *subsumption*, which had been introduced by Robinson (1965: sect. 7.2, pp. 38–9), to obtain a partial ordering of the clauses in terms of generality. This was then used to define what he called a r.l.g.g. (relative least general generalization). These ideas play a crucial role in GOLEM. So I will now briefly explain them.

Let C, D be clauses.[9] Suppose θ is a substitution which replaces the variables of C by terms to produce a new clause $C\theta$. If for some such θ, we have that $C\theta \subseteq D$, then C is said to *subsume* D. This defines a partial ordering of the clauses in terms of greater or less generality, and, using this ordering, we can define the least general generalization (l.g.g.) C of two clauses D_1 and D_2. For the purposes of inductive inference, it is more important to consider what is called the relative least general generalization (r.l.g.g.) of two data points e_1 and e_2. The data points are represented as ground atoms of the clausal logic, and their l.g.g. is relativized to some background knowledge K. More precisely, clause C is said to be the least general generalization of e_1 and e_2 relative to K whenever C is the least general clause in the partial ordering of the clauses for which K&C entails e_1&e_2, where C is used only once in the derivation of both e_1 and e_2. Muggleton and Feng (1992: 284–5) give a method for constructing the r.l.g.g. of two clauses, and then generalize it to n clauses. The details of the construction need not concern us, but it is worth pointing out one feature. To make the construction work, the background knowledge K has to be expressed in the form of a finite set of ground atoms. So, in machine-learning programs which use this construction, it is not possible to make direct use of background knowledge in the form of laws and generalizations. Such laws have to be replaced by a finite conjunction of singular instances. This is obviously a defect in the general method,[10] but there are some situations—for example, the protein structure problem which will be considered in Section 2.6—where the representation of background knowledge in the form of a finite conjunction of singular statements is by no means inconvenient.

The construction of a relative least general generalization certainly seems promising as part of a basic inductive rule of inference for a machine-learning system. However, having introduced the notion, Plotkin encountered a problem. His r.l.g.g.'s could in the worst case contain infinitely many literals, and in general tended to grow exponentially with the number of examples involved. For these reasons the approach was abandoned until it was taken up again by Muggleton and Feng. They managed to introduce restrictions which caused the resulting r.l.g.g.'s to be not just finite, but of a reasonable length. Using such r.l.g.g.'s it was possible to construct a machine-learning program (GOLEM) operating according to the following iterative procedure.

GOLEM is provided with a set of positive examples and a set of negative examples. It begins by taking a random sample of pairs of positive examples. It constructs the r.l.g.g. of each such pair. GOLEM takes each such r.l.g.g. and computes the number of examples which it could be used to predict. Clearly a given r.l.g.g. might predict some examples which are false. GOLEM therefore chooses the r.l.g.g. which predicts the most true examples while predicting less than a predefined threshold of false examples. Having found the pair with the best r.l.g.g. (S, say), GOLEM then takes a further random sample of the as yet unpredicted positive examples, and forms the r.l.g.g of S and each of the members of this new random sample. These new r.l.g.g.'s are evaluated as before, and the process continues until no improvement in prediction is produced.

It is clear that this procedure is bottom up in character. GOLEM generalizes cautiously from two data points by forming their r.l.g.g. From a set of r.l.g.g.'s, the one with the widest cover is chosen, and it is then extended cautiously by forming the r.l.g.g. with an augmented set containing a data point as yet unpredicted, and so on. In this way generalizations are gradually extended to cover more and more examples.

The GOLEM algorithm also fits neatly into our framework of IRIs and falsifications. The basic IRI consists in forming the r.l.g.g. of a finite set of positive examples. As the construction of the r.l.g.g. explicitly involves the background knowledge K (in the form of a finite conjunction of singular statements), this IRI fits our scheme of H = f(K,e). Those r.l.g.g.'s which predict more than a predefined number of negative examples are eliminated as 'falsified'. Thus falsification plays a role in the iteration procedure.

Like ID3, and indeed any practical machine-learning system, GOLEM needs a method for dealing with noisy data. An interesting approach was developed using a measure of the extent to which a proposed theory compresses the data. A compression measure was suggested by Muggleton (1988), and developed into a way of handling noise in Srinivasan, Muggleton, and Bain (1994). Each hypothesis produced by GOLEM in the experimentation stage is checked by compression for significance before it is accepted for further consideration. Experimental results show that this allows GOLEM to handle noisy data quite satisfactorily.

2.5. Bratko's Summary of the Successes of Machine Learning in the Turing Tradition, 1992

We have examined two important machine-learning systems developed in the Turing tradition. It is now time to consider what successes these and related systems have had in dealing with Feigenbaum's bottleneck. In June 1992 Ivan Bratko presented a summary of results which had been attained in this direction at the International Conference on Fifth Generation Computer Systems in Tokyo, Japan. I will here present a brief summary of his paper (Bratko 1992), which is indeed striking and impressive.

Ivan Bratko from Slovenia is another leading researcher in the Turing tradition. In the 1980s he spent a good deal of time working with Donald Michie in Edinburgh or Glasgow, and now heads an important research group in Slovenia. He and his group have introduced several important machine-learning systems. One of these (ASSISTANT) was developed from Quinlan's ID3. It belongs to the

TDIDT (Top-Down Induction of Decision Trees) family, but, relative to ID3, incorporates many changes and new features. The results reported by Bratko were for the most part obtained either with ASSISTANT or with GOLEM.

It will be remembered that Feigenbaum's bottleneck arose because of the great length of time needed to obtain rules for expert systems by interviewing domain experts. Bratko points out, however, that it may not just be a matter of time. In some cases, it may simply be impossible to obtain rules from the domain experts, because these experts, although they can perform the task satisfactorily, may have no conscious knowledge of how they do so. In such cases machine-learning (ML) techniques may be necessary to produce an expert system at all. Bratko quotes an interesting case of this sort in his paper. It bears some resemblance to Michie's apocryphal tale of the Camembert sampler, which I quoted earlier (Sect. 2.2). Bratko's story concerns the Jesenice Steel Mill in Slovenia. This is what he says:

A review . . . 1991 . . . of AI applications done by my laboratory in Ljubljana . . . contains many applications with similar scenario. Among over sixty AI applications included in the review, almost half of them critically rely on the use of ML techniques. One more or less randomly chosen example . . . is from the Jesenice Steel Mill, Slovenia. Their problem was the control of the quality of the rolling emulsion for the Sendzimir rolling mill. The quality of rolling critically depends on the properties of emulsion. An expert therefore daily measured various parameters of emulsion in the rolling mill (concentration of iron, ashes, presence of bacteria, etc.) and decided on the appropriate action (e.g. change emulsion, add anti-bacteria oil, no action, etc.). When the expert was expected to leave the company they attempted to construct an expert system, extracting his decision knowledge from him in the dialogue fashion. Only when after half a year there was no clear progress, they were prepared to apply a ML tool (Assistant Professional in this case . . .) using example decisions from the expert's practice as learning examples. The resulting decision tree, implemented as an expert system, is now used regularly and completely substitutes the decisions that were previously made by the expert. (Bratko 1992: 1208)

Apart from demonstrating the need for machine-learning techniques, this example gives an indication of the enormous impact expert systems technology is likely to have on production processes.

Bratko next turns to the field of medical diagnosis, where the accuracy of machine diagnosis using rules obtained by mechanical induction can be compared to the accuracy of medical specialists.

Table 2.1. Diagnoses by human specialists and ASSISTANT

Domain	Human specialists	ASSISTANT
lymphography 1		76%
lymphography 2		65%
primary tumour	42%, 1.22 bit	44%, 1.38 bit
breast cancer	64%, 0.05 bit	77%, 0.07 bit
hepatitis		83%
thyroid	64%, 0.59 bit	73%, 0.86 bit
rheumatology	56%, 0.26 bit	61%, 0.46 bit
urinary tract m		70%
urinary tract f		80%

The procedure was to choose randomly 70 per cent of the available data for learning, and then diagnose the remaining 30 per cent using the rule obtained. The system's diagnoses were then compared with physician's diagnoses on the same data. The cases were such that the true condition of the patient had eventually been found. This procedure was repeated several times (usually ten times) to reduce statistical fluctuations, and the average taken.

Bratko gives results for several systems, but in Table 2.1 I will present only those for his system ASSISTANT mentioned earlier. For each disease category, the table gives the percentage of correct diagnoses by the human specialists, and by ASSISTANT. In some cases, Bratko also gives an information score in bits for the diagnosis. This measures the extent to which the human (or system) does better than the uninformed classifier, who always assigns the patient to the majority class. Such a classifier has a zero information score, and the higher the information score the better the performance. What is striking here is that ASSISTANT did better than the human specialists on all the cases on which an objective statistical comparison was possible, and on both of the measures used. As Bratko remarks: 'One conclusion . . . is that the knowledge bases induced from no more than a few hundreds of examples of patients in some narrow diagnostic domain, perform better than medical doctors, including best specialists. Such a conclusion has been empirically confirmed by several other studies' (1992: 1210). He adds, however, the following caveat—perhaps to mollify the sensibilities of the medical profession:

This result should, of course, be taken with some qualifications. Namely, the criterion here is only in terms of classification accuracy (or information score) under the condition that both the human expert and the induced classifier are given the same information. In practice, the human expert might be able to use extra information. Also, the medical doctor would typically have a much better global understanding of the problem and be capable of deeper explanation of the particular cases. (Bratko 1992: 1210)

So far Bratko's examples have all used attribute-based learning systems, but he next considers a case where a relational learning system was used. This is the problem of finite-element mesh design. As we proceed with the description of this problem, it will become clear why attribute-based learning is inadequate in this case, and a relational learning system is needed. In fact three relational learning algorithms were tried on the problem, namely: FOIL, GOLEM, and LINUS. As GOLEM gave the best results, it is the one whose use is described by Bratko. Some of the work using GOLEM on this problem was carried out jointly by Dolšak, a member of Bratko's group, and Muggleton. They give an account of their procedure in Dolšak and Muggleton (1992). I will base my account on this paper as well as Bratko's.

The finite-element mesh design problem arises in situations in which engineers are trying to analyse stresses in physical structures such as a cylinder from a hydraulic press used in the leather industry (see Fig. 2.4). The modelling technique used is to divide the structure into a finite number of elements, and then use a linear approximation to the mechanical equations to calculate the stresses in each element. The size of the mesh used is not the same at every point of the structure. Fine meshes are used at critical points where there may be high stresses, and coarser meshes elsewhere (see Fig. 2.5). The finer the mesh, the more accurate the results obtained, but also the longer and more expensive the computer time needed for the calculations. The problem then is to find the coarsest mesh which will produce sufficiently accurate results. Expert users of finite-element methods can make good guesses about the proper density of the mesh in various regions of the object. However, as usual, they have great difficulty in formulating rules for making such guesses. Here, then, is a typical case in which machine-learning methods have a role in discovering the rules which are needed.

Dolšak and Muggleton tackled the problem by considering the structure as a collection of edges. In a training example provided by an expert, the appropriate number of finite elements along each edge was given. This varied between 1 and 17. A list of labelled edges with the number of its partition provided the positive examples. By

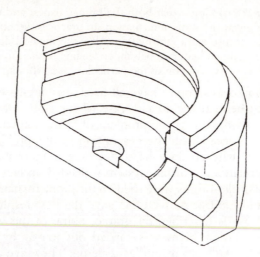

Fig. 2.4. A typical structure to be analysed
Source: Dolšak and Muggleton (1992: 454)

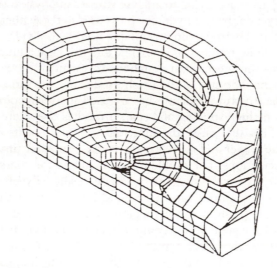

Fig. 2.5. Finite-element mesh for the structure
Source: Dolšak and Muggleton (1992: 455)

simply varying the number of the partition from that provided by the expert, a set of negative examples was obtained. The problem was perhaps well suited to GOLEM, because the background knowledge could easily be formulated as a set of singular statements. For example, each edge of a given training structure could be described in terms of its length as short, usual length, long. It could further be stated what shape the edge had, whether it was loaded or not loaded, and so on. In this way, the relevant background knowledge about the structure could be stated as a list of singular statements about its edges. In the example cited by Bratko, training meshes were provided by experts for five structures, and these yielded 357 positive examples, 2,840 negative examples, and 2,132 background facts.

GOLEM got to work on this data and produced a number of rules. One of them, if translated into English, runs as follows. The appropriate partitioning of an arbitrary edge (EdgeX, say) is 7 if EdgeX is of the usual length, has a neighbour EdgeY in the xy-plane such that EdgeY is fixed at both ends, and has a neighbour EdgeZ in the xz-plane such that EdgeZ is not loaded. To formulate this rule we need to use the 2-place relation of neighbourhood. Thus we have to say that EdgeX is a neighbour of EdgeY in the xy-plane, or, in symbols, neighbour_xy(EdgeX, EdgeY). neighbour_xy is a 2-place predicate, so that it could not be expressed in an attribute-based system which uses only 1-place predicates. The rule induced is also a Horn clause of the kind used in PROLOG. For these reasons, a relational learning system was clearly necessary and appropriate for this case.

One interesting point to note here is that a rule induced by GOLEM can be considered and evaluated by a domain expert, even by one who was completely incapable of formulating rules on his or her own. The domain expert would be in a position to understand and comment on the rule, and perhaps to learn something from it. We have here an important human–computer interaction, which will be discussed a little further in the next section.

The rules induced by GOLEM were not able, entirely on their own, to generate a satisfactory mesh for an entirely new structure. They were able to do so, but only with the help of an automatic mesh generator, and some corrections introduced by a human rule of thumb. None the less the advance achieved in the problem is striking and significant.

2.6. GOLEM's Discovery of a Law of Nature

So far we have considered the use of machine-learning systems for generating the rules needed for expert systems. However, it is also possible to use these systems in scientific investigations. The ancient Greek philosopher Democritus remarked that he would 'rather discover one cause than gain the kingdom of Persia' (Diels, Fragment 118; quoted from Freeman 1947: 104). If GOLEM were a conscious being, and shared the tastes of Democritus, then it would enjoy more felicity than becoming the King of Persia could have brought, since, in one investigation, it discovered what could justly be claimed to be a causal law of nature.[11] Admittedly this law of nature is rather low level, and is certainly not as exciting as, for example, Kepler's laws. However, it is indeed a law of nature, and was not known to the scientists working in the field before GOLEM's efforts. Moreover, the field in question is one of the most important and exciting in modern science.

GOLEM was set to work on an investigation of protein structure. A good introduction to this field is Branden and Tooze (1991), while GOLEM's contribution is described in Muggleton, King, and Sternberg (1992). Twenty different amino acids constitute the building blocks of all proteins. These are joined end to end, so that a protein consists of a sequence of amino acid residues. Now it is relatively easy to discover the sequence of residues in a protein. This is known as the protein's *primary structure*. Unfortunately, knowledge of the primary structure of a protein is not sufficient to understand the biological properties of the protein, for these depend crucially on the three-dimensional shape of the protein. Now proteins as they form fold up into complicated three-dimensional structures, which are known as the protein's *secondary structure*. The secondary structure of a protein can be determined by X-ray crystallography or NMR (nuclear magnetic resonance) techniques; but it is a long and costly business. So far the secondary structures of about 500 proteins have been determined. Progress in biochemistry would become much easier and quicker if it were possible to predict the secondary structure of a protein (which is difficult to determine but biologically crucial) from the primary structure (which is easy to determine but not so significant biologically). As Branden and Tooze put it: 'To understand the biological function of proteins we should therefore like to be able to deduce or predict the three-dimensional structure from the amino acid sequence. This we cannot do. In spite of considerable efforts over the last 25 years, this folding problem is still unsolved and remains one of the most basic intellectual challenges in molecular biology' (1991: 3). Machine-learning techniques have advanced to the point at which they can make a contribution to one of the leading problems of modern natural science.

Substructures of a protein structure are usually of one of two basic types: α-*helices* and β-*strands*. α-helices were first described in 1951 by Linus Pauling, who predicted that such a structure would be stable and favourable in proteins. This remarkable prediction almost immediately received strong experimental support from diffraction patterns obtained by Max Perrutz in Cambridge. Proteins can accordingly be classified into three domains according to their secondary structure. These are (i) alpha-type domains, in which the proteins have only α-helices (or at least have very few β-strands), (ii) beta-type domains, and (iii) alpha/beta-type domains, where α-helices alternate with β-strands. The simplest prediction problem is obtained by restricting the proteins considered to those of alpha-type domain, and then attempting to predict from the primary structure whether a particular residue belongs to an α-helix or not.

GOLEM was applied to this problem in the following fashion. Twelve non-homologous proteins of known structure and alpha-type domain, involving 1,612 residues, were selected as the training set. From this training set and background knowledge, GOLEM learned a small set of rules for predicting which residues are part of α-helices. The rules were then tested on four independent non-homologous proteins of known structure and alpha-type domain, involving 416 residues. The accuracy of the rules was 81 per cent (± 2 per cent). These then were the overall procedure and results. We shall next examine in more detail how the problem was coded into GOLEM, and one of the rules which GOLEM discovered.

The positive and negative examples were coded by means of a 2-place predicate: alpha (Protein name, Position), e.g. alpha (155C, 105). This says that residue 105 in protein 155C is an α-helix. The negative examples are obtained by stating in the same way that a residue of a particular protein is an α-helix, when in fact it is not. We now come to the crucial background knowledge. Each residue can be described in terms of properties which are recognized by scientists in the field to be relevant to the question of the protein's secondary structure. These include the size of the residue (e.g. small), its hydrophobicity, whether it is polar, whether it is aromatic, and so on. Two-place predicates giving information about the relations between residues were also used (e.g. Ith (X,Y) meaning that X is less hydrophobic than Y).

The background knowledge also included predicates whose purpose was to determine the kinds of generalization which GOLEM would consider. A typical example was a predicate octf describing nine sequential positions (e.g. octf (19, 20, 21, 22, 23, 24, 25, 26, 27)). This enabled GOLEM to search for laws in which the character of a particular residue (whether it belonged to an α-helix or not) would be determined by the basic properties of the residue itself, and of the four residues on each side of it. Indeed the law which we shall consider later is of something like this form. Two points are worth noting here. First of all, providing GOLEM with this particular predicate in the background knowledge is clearly equivalent to giving it a heuristic to guide its search. Once again we can see the equivalence of heuristics with background knowledge/assumptions. Secondly, it was pointed out earlier that GOLEM can use background knowledge only in the form of singular statements, or basic facts, and not in the form of generalizations. Thus a general definition of a sequence of nine consecutive positions cannot be given, and, instead, all such sequences have to be listed in the form given above. In general, this would be very inconvenient, but, as a protein consists of a relatively small finite number of residues, there is no problem in this case. This shows that the protein structure problem is particularly suitable for GOLEM.

In the same way, the background knowledge contains the 3-place predicate alpha_triplet (X, Y, Z), which holds when $Y = X + 1$, and $Z = X + 4$, e.g. alpha_triplet (5, 6, 9). This is because in an α-helix these residues appear on the same face of the helix, and so the introduction of this predicate allows GOLEM to make a preferential search for common relationships between these residues. For the same reason, some 2-place predicates such as alpha_pair (X, Y), which holds when $Y = X + 3$, and alpha_pair 4(X, Y), which holds when $Y = X + 4$, are introduced.

GOLEM searched for its rules in an iterative fashion. The rules found on the first run were added to the background knowledge, and the program was run again. The effect of this is described by Muggleton, King, and Sternberg as follows:

The predicted secondary structure positions found using the first rules (level 0 rules) were added to the background information . . . and then

Golem was re-run to produce new rules (level 1 rules). This forms a kind of bootstrapping learning process, with the output of a lower level of rules providing the input for the next level. This was needed because after the level 0 rules, the predictions made were quite speckled, i.e. only short sequences of α-helix predicted residues interspersed by predictions of coil secondary structure. The level 1 rules have the effect of filtering the speckled prediction and joining together the short sequences of α-helix predictions. The iterative learning process was repeated a second time, with the predicted secondary structure positions from the level 1 rules being added to the background information, and new rules found (level 2 rules). The level 2 rules had the effect of reducing the speckling even more and clumping together sequences of α-helix. Some of the level 1 and 2 rules were finally generalized by hand with the formation of the symmetrical variants of the rules found by Golem. (Muggleton, King, and Sternberg 1992: 650)

Let us now look at one of the rules produced by GOLEM. I have selected Rule 12, which is a level 0 rule, and so was generated by GOLEM from the initial background knowledge. The rule is stated in PROLOG format by Muggleton, King, and Sternberg (1992: 655). If translated into something closer to normal English, it runs as follows:

GOLEM'S Rule 12 regarding Protein Secondary Structure
There is an α-helix residue in protein A at position B if

  (i) the residue at B–2 is not proline,
 (ii) the residue at B–1 is neither aromatic nor proline,
(iii) the residue at B is large, not aromatic, and not lysine,
 (iv) the residue at B+1 is hydrophobic and not lysine,
  (v) the residue at B+2 is neither aromatic nor proline,
 (vi) the residue at B+3 is neither aromatic nor proline, and either small or polar, and
(vii) the residue at B+4 is hydrophobic and not lysine.

Some readers may feel rather disappointed with this rule, which is rather long, cumbersome, and specific. It was, however, 95 per cent accurate on the training set, and 81 per cent accurate on the test set. It was not known before being produced by GOLEM, and it makes a contribution to an important current problem in the natural sciences. It seems to me fair, therefore, to credit GOLEM with the discovery of a law of nature.

Muggleton, King, and Sternberg make the following interesting comments on GOLEM's rules, and on Rule 12 in particular:

Machine Learning in the Turing Tradition

The rules generated by Golem can be considered to be hypotheses about the way α-helices form . . . They define patterns of relationships which, if they exist in a sequence of residues, will tend to cause a specified residue to form part of an α-helix. For example, considering rule 12, this rule specifies the properties of eight sequential residues which, if held, will cause the middle residue in sequence (residue B) to form part of a helix. These rules are of particular interest because they were generated automatically and do not reflect any preconceived ideas about possible rule form (except those unavoidably built into the selection of background information). The rules raise many questions about α-helix formation. Considering rule 12, the residue p (proline) is disallowed in a number of positions, but allowed in others—yet proline is normally considered to disrupt proteins. (Muggleton, King, and Sternberg 1992: 656)

There are a number of observations which can be made about this passage. First of all, in sentences two and three, the authors speak appropriately of a pattern of relationships which, if they exist, 'will cause the middle residue in the sequence . . . to form part of a helix'. This justifies regarding Rule 12 as a causal law of nature, and so our earlier claim that GOLEM has discovered such a law. The last two sentences of the passage are also important, because they show that it is possible to study the rules generated by a machine-learning programme, and that such rules can generate new insights into the subject. Indeed, Donald Michie and others working in the Turing tradition of machine learning have always stressed the desirability of producing rules which are humanly comprehensible. This is another advantage of the PROLOG formalism, since PROLOG rules can usually be translated into understandable English quite easily. The same is sometimes true of decision trees, but not always. It is possible for a complicated decision tree to be generated mechanically which works well in a particular domain, but is incomprehensible to a domain expert. Quinlan is aware of this problem, and in his 1986 paper discusses a method suggested by Alan Shapiro for overcoming it. This method works in at least some cases, for, as Quinlan says: 'In one classification problem studied, this method reduced a totally opaque, large decision tree to a hierarchy of nine small decision trees, each of which "made sense" to an expert' (1986: 104). At all events, there are great advantages in generating rules which are humanly comprehensible, because this allows the following kind of human–machine interaction. Background knowledge supplied by the human scientist is coded into a machine-learning program. This generates hitherto unknown, but humanly comprehensible, rules which apply in the domain in question. The human scientist can then examine these rules, and perhaps obtain new insights into the field.

From this perspective, machine-learning systems can be seen, not as replacements for the human scientist, but as new tools for the human scientist to use—tools which may powerfully assist his or her quest for knowledge. Later on (in Chapter 6), I will argue more generally that this is the correct perspective with which to view advances in artificial intelligence. In the next chapter (Chapter 3), I will consider the rather more specific question of how the advances in machine learning described in this chapter affect theories of scientific method.

3 How Advances in Machine Learning Affect the Inductivist Controversy

HAVING given an account of some advances in machine learning in the Turing tradition, I will now turn to the question of how these affect the inductivist controversy. There can be no doubt that the results described tend, on the whole, to support Bacon and undermine Popper. I have already quoted Popper's emphatic statement: 'Induction, i.e. inference based on many observations, is a myth. It is neither a psychological fact, nor a fact of ordinary life, nor one of scientific procedure' (Popper 1963: 53).

This view can no longer be maintained in the light of programs such as ID3 or GOLEM which do make inductive inferences based on many observations and have become a part of scientific procedure.

Despite this blow to some of Popper's more extreme claims, it by no means follows that the new results are all and unequivocally in favour of Bacon against Popper. On the contrary, some of Popper's ideas do find support from the advances in machine learning. Later in the chapter, I will consider some of the points that could be made in Popper's favour, but it is more natural to start by considering Bacon, whose ideas have received a remarkable, and to some extent unexpected, vindication from the advances in machine learning. In the next section, we shall look rather more closely at Bacon's detailed description of how induction should be carried out, and it will become clear that many of his ideas have actually been incorporated in the successful machine-learning programs.

3.1. Bacon's Example of Heat

In the *Novum Organum* Bacon illustrates his new method of induction by giving a detailed investigation of the nature (or, as he says, 'Form') of heat. The first part of this yields what Bacon calls, alluding to his wine-making analogy, the *First Vintage concerning the Form of Heat*. It is contained in the second book of the *Novum Organum*, sections X to XX. Bacon begins in section X by giving an outline of his method, which involves three steps. The first is the formation of what he calls a *Natural and Experimental History*. This is, in effect, the collection of observations, and carrying-out of experiments relating to the subject in hand. The next step is the arrangement of these observations and experimental results in *Tables*, and the third step is of course the application of *Induction* to these tables to yield scientific results. As Bacon himself says:

For first of all we must prepare a *Natural and Experimental History*, sufficient and good; and this is the foundation of all; for we are not to imagine or suppose, but to discover, what nature does or may be made to do.

But natural and experimental history is so various and diffuse, that it confounds and distracts the understanding, unless it be ranged and presented to view in a suitable order. We must therefore form *Tables and Arrangements of Instances*, in such a method and order that the understanding may be able to deal with them.

And even when this is done, still the understanding, if left to itself and its own spontaneous movements, is incompetent and unfit to form axioms, unless it be directed and guarded. Therefore in the third place we must use *Induction*, true and legitimate induction, which is the very key of interpretation. (Bacon 1620: 307)

In his investigation of heat, Bacon begins by presenting what he calls a *Table of Essence and Presence*, which consists of *Instances agreeing in the Nature of Heat*—that is to say, of examples in which heat is present. In all, Bacon gives twenty-seven instances, and adds 'other instances' as number 28. To illustrate his approach, I will give eight of his instances:

1. The rays of the sun, especially in summer and at noon.
6. All flame.
9. Liquids boiling or heated.
14. All bodies, whether solid or liquid, whether dense or rare (as the air itself is), held for a time near the fire.

16. All bodies rubbed violently, as stone, wood, cloth, etc., insomuch that poles and axles of wheels sometimes catch fire; and the way they kindled fire in the West Indies was by attrition.
18. Quick lime sprinkled with water.
19. Iron, when first dissolved by strong waters in glass, and that without being put near the fire. And in like manner tin, etc., but not with equal intensity.
20. Animals. especially and at all times internally; though in insects the heat is not perceptible to the touch by reason of the smallness of their size. (Bacon 1620: 308)

Having given this table of instances where heat is present, Bacon goes on to compile a table of instances where heat is absent. However, he does this guided by his first table. For each instance of the first table, he tries to find an instance as similar as possible, but in which heat is absent. Thus he calls the result a Table of Deviation, or of Absence in Proximity, and says that it contains Instances in Proximity where the Nature of Heat is Absent. Corresponding to number 1 (the heat of the sun), we have: 'The rays of the moon and of stars and comets are not found to be hot to the touch; indeed the severest colds are observed to be at full moons' (Bacon 1620: 309).

I will now go through Bacon's instances of absence in proximity, corresponding to the other seven examples taken from his table of presence:

[Corresponding to 6] All flame is in all cases more or less warm; nor is there any Negative to be subjoined. And yet they say that the *ignis fatuus* (as it is called), which sometimes even settles on a wall, has not much heat . . .

[Corresponding to 9] To warm liquids I subjoin the Negative Instance of liquid itself in its natural state. For we find no tangible liquid which is warm in its own nature and remains so constantly; but the warmth is an adventitious nature, superinduced only for the time being . . .

[Corresponding to 14] To this no Negative is subjoined. For there is nothing found among us either tangible or spirituous which does not contract warmth when put near fire.

[Corresponding to 16] There is no Negative, I think, to be subjoined to this Instance. For we find among us no tangible body which does not manifestly gain warmth by attrition . . .

[Corresponding to 18] On this Instance too should be made more diligent inquiry. For quick lime sprinkled with water seems to contract heat, either by the concentration of heat before dispersed . . ., or because the igneous spirit is irritated and exasperated by the water, so as to cause a conflict and reaction. Which of these two is the real cause will more readily appear if oil be poured on instead of water; for oil will serve equally well with water to concentrate the enclosed spirit, but not to irritate it. We should also extend the experiment both by employing the ashes and rusts of different bodies, and by pouring in different liquids. [Here, and in many other cases, Bacon proposes that existing observations should be augmented by making a series of experiments.]

[Corresponding to 19] To this Instance is subjoined the Negative of other metals which are softer and more fusible. For gold-leaf dissolved by aqua regia gives no heat to the touch; no more does lead dissolved in aqua fortis; neither again does quicksilver (as I remember) . . .

[Corresponding to 20] To the heat of animals no Negative is subjoined, except that of insects (as above-mentioned), on account of their small size. For in fishes, as compared with land animals, it is rather a low degree than an absence of heat that is noted. But in vegetables and plants there is no degree of heat perceptible to the touch, either in their exudations or in their pith when freshly exposed. (Bacon 1620: 311–14)

Bacon next constructs a third table, which is called a *Table of Degrees or Comparison in Heat*. The idea here is to compare variations in heat either in the same subject, or between different subjects. Bacon gives forty-one instances which are not arranged in any particular order. They can be illustrated by number 27, which runs as follows: 'Motion increases heat, as you may see in bellows, and by blowing; insomuch that the harder metals are not dissolved or melted by a dead or quiet fire, till it be made intense by blowing' (Bacon 1620: 318).

The three tables, taken together, are called by Bacon the 'Presentation of Instances to the Understanding'. Once the 'Instances' are presented, the method of induction must be applied to obtain the form of heat. We will now examine what Bacon says about this.

Bacon's induction begins with the process of *Exclusion, or Rejection of Natures from the Form of Heat*. Let us call a particular nature A. If we can find an instance in the first table where heat is present, but A absent, it follows that the existence of heat does not imply A. Conversely, if we can find an instance in the second table where A is present, but heat absent, it follows that the existence of A does not imply heat. Using arguments of this kind, Bacon excludes and rejects lightness and brightness, because the rays of the moon are light and bright without being hot, while iron can become very hot without being light and bright. Similarly he rejects rarity, on the grounds that gold can be hot without becoming rare, while air is always rare, but is often very cold. Thus he says:

6. On account of the rays of the moon and other heavenly bodies, with the exception of the sun, also reject lightness and brightness.
7. By a comparison of ignited iron and the flame of spirit of wine (of which ignited iron has more heat and less brightness, while the flame of spirit of wine has more brightness and less heat), also reject light and brightness.
8. On account of ignited gold and other metals, which are of the greatest density as a whole, reject rarity.
9. On account of air, which is found for the most part cold and yet remains rare, also reject rarity. (Bacon 1620: 322)

Bacon gives fourteen examples of this sort.

The process of exclusion and rejection, given the tables, is relatively routine and mechanical, and, as I will argue in the next section, Bacon probably hoped that this process would lead to a single definite result. This did not happen in his example of heat, however, and he was therefore forced, in order to obtain his 'First Vintage', to adopt what he called 'the affirmative way'. He more or less admits that this may lead to error, thereby implying that it is rather conjectural, and we may add that the process appears to be somewhat intuitive and creative rather than routine and mechanical, as Bacon himself would wish. Bacon introduces his 'affirmative way' in the following rather apologetic fashion: 'And yet since truth will sooner come out from error than from confusion, I think it expedient that the understanding should have permission, after the three Tables of First Presentation (such as I have exhibited) have been made and weighed, to make an essay of the Interpretation of Nature in the affirmative way . . .' (1620: 323). Bacon first argues that Heat must be a special case of motion. As he says:

From a survey of the instances, all and each, the nature of which Heat is a particular case appears to be Motion. This is displayed most conspicuously in flame, which is always in motion, and in boiling or simmering liquids, which also are in perpetual motion. It is also shown in the excitement or increase of heat caused by motion, as in bellows and blasts . . . It is shown also by this, that all bodies are destroyed, or at any rate notably altered by all strong and vehement fire and heat; whence it is quite clear that heat causes a tumult and confusion and violent motion in the internal parts of a body which perceptibly tends to its dissolution. (Bacon 1620: 323)

Bacon next argues that heat is not a motion of the body as a whole, but of its smaller parts. He thus arrives at his famous conclusion:

'Now from this our First Vintage it follows that the Form or true definition of heat (heat, that is, in relation to the universe, not simply in relation to man) is in few words as follows: *Heat is a motion, expansive, restrained, and acting in its strife upon the smaller particles of bodies*' (Bacon 1620: 325–6).

After concluding his 'First Vintage', Bacon goes on to develop his theory of induction further, but I will not follow him in this. The 'First Vintage' already contains what is perhaps the most substantial part of his method of induction, and it will, therefore, be convenient now to assess its scientific worth, and to see how it relates to the machine-learning programs described in the previous chapter.

Any unprejudiced reader must, I think, agree that Bacon's investigation of heat is a considerable scientific achievement for its time. Bacon's conclusion that heat is the motion of the small particles of a body is in substantial agreement with the kinetic theory of heat accepted today. This is all the more remarkable because right up to the beginning of the nineteenth century the erroneous caloric theory, according to which heat is a material fluid, prevailed in scientific circles. Moreover, Bacon's success cannot be dismissed as due merely to luck, for it does seem to have some connection with his method. In particular he mentions in his Table 1 (of Essence and Presence), instance 16, the fact that heat is produced by friction. This was later to be one of the key arguments in favour of the kinetic theory. For example, in his famous experiment of 1798, designed to attack the caloric theory, Count Rumford showed that an indefinitely large quantity of heat can be produced in boring cannon.

Another noteworthy point is that many of the instances which Bacon cites in his tables proved to be of crucial importance in the much later chemical revolution, which led to Lavoisier's oxygen theory. The following are examples. The discussion of the effect of water on quick lime at 18 in Table 1 with the suggested experiments in the corresponding instance of Table 2; related experimental investigations led to Joseph Black's discovery of carbon dioxide (or 'fixed air', as it was initially called); this was published in Black's *Experiments on Magnesia Alba, Quick-lime and Some Other Alcaline Substances* of 1756. The effect of acids on metals mentioned in Tables 1, 19, and the commentary in Table 2, the discussion of animal heat in Tables 1, 20, and the commentary in Table 2, and the mention of the effect of bellows on fire in Tables 3, 27 are all phenomena, the discussion of which played an important part in Lavoisier's thinking. This is not, of course, to say that Bacon anticipated Lavoisier, only that Bacon's list of observations and experiments contained much of great scientific importance.

Let us now examine how Bacon's method of induction, as displayed in his 'First Vintage concerning the Form of Heat', relates to the modern machine-learning programs described in the previous chapter. As we saw, Hunt *et al.* in their 1966 book, one of the pioneering works of machine learning, used the distinction between positive and negative instances, and this distinction was adopted in all the subsequent machine-learning programs considered in the chapter. Now clearly this distinction is exactly that between Bacon's Tables 1 and 2. Indeed Bacon actually uses the term 'Negative Instance' in his exposition of Table 2 in section XII, p. 312. However, the correspondence with Bacon's ideas goes further. Bacon, it will be remembered, constructs his Table 2 from Table 1 by seeking, for each positive instance of Table 1, an instance in Table 2 which is similar and yet negative. In the two applications of GOLEM which we considered in Chapter 2, Muggleton and his fellow workers also constructed the set of negative examples from the positive examples. Thus, in the finite-element mesh example, the positive examples were taken from meshes which had been constructed by experts. The set of positive examples consisted of a list of labelled edges, each paired with the number of its partition which had been assigned by the expert. The negative examples were then generated simply by changing the number of the partition of each labelled edge to a different value from that provided by the expert. Similarly in the protein-folding example, the positive examples were obtained from proteins whose three-dimensional structure was known. This generated a series of positive examples which stated that a particular residue in a particular protein was part of an α-helix. The negative examples were then generated by stating that a particular residue in a particular protein was part of an α-helix, when in fact it was not.

These examples may, of course, simply be cases of different people coming up with similar ideas when studying similar problems. However, some more direct influence of Bacon on recent work in artificial intelligence is not to be excluded. Indeed Muggleton in his 1988 paper makes an explicit reference to Bacon's *Novum Organum*. The paper is concerned with developing the machine-learning program CIGOL (i.e. LOGIC spelt backwards), which was a predecessor of GOLEM. In section 4 of the paper, Muggleton gives details of the performance of a revised version of CIGOL in an investigation of the properties of light, which Muggleton describes as 'in the spirit of Bacon's exposition'. This is a truly remarkable example of a book of 1620 influencing a hi-tech development of the late twentieth century.

So far then we have shown how developments in machine learning have given support to Bacon's views on scientific method, and undermined Popper's approach. This is not the whole story, however, and something can be said on Popper's side as well. This will be done in the next three sections, which make some points favourable to Popper, without, however, necessarily detracting from Bacon's achievement.

3.2. The Importance of Falsification

Popper is known above all for the stress he lays on the importance of falsification (or refutation) of scientific hypotheses. Now in all the machine-learning programs we considered, falsification played a crucial role. Typically the program generated a hypothesis from some data and the background knowledge. This hypothesis was then tested out against data and, if refuted by the data, was replaced by a new or modified hypothesis. Such repeated sequences of conjectures and refutations played a crucial role in all the machine-learning programs, and, in this respect, they agreed with Popper's methodology, except, of course, that the conjectures were generated mechanically by the program rather than intuitively by humans.

This vindication of Popper turns out to be a further vindication of Bacon as well. When I gave my introductory account of the views of Bacon and Popper in Chapter 1, I stressed those points on which the two philosophers disagreed, but, as I mentioned at the time, there are some other points on which they hold the same or similar opinions. One of these is the importance of falsification, for Bacon stresses the need for falsification and considers the process of falsification to be an essential part of his inductive method.

In the plan of the *Novum Organum*, Bacon gives the following preliminary account of his new method of induction.

But the greatest change I introduce is in the form itself of induction and the judgement made thereby. For the induction of which the logicians speak, which proceeds by simple enumeration, is a puerile thing; concludes at hazard; is always liable to be upset by a contradictory instance; takes into account only what is known and ordinary; and leads to no result.

Now what the sciences stand in need of is a form of induction which shall analyse experience and take it to pieces, and by a due process of exclusion and rejection lead to an inevitable conclusion. (1620: 249)

Induction by simple enumeration is the process by which a generalization (or prediction) is inductively inferred from the observation of a large number of similar instances. Thus, to take the standard example, from the observation of several thousand white swans, it might be inferred inductively (by simple enumeration) either that all swans are white (generalization), or that the next swan to be encountered will be white (prediction). Now Bacon regards this kind of induction as 'a puerile thing', and stresses that his form of induction will be based on 'exclusion and rejection' (his terms for Popper's 'falsification and refutation'). It is also worth noting that Bacon thinks that 'a due process of exclusion and rejection' will 'lead to an inevitable conclusion'. This is a point to which I will return in a moment.

When Bacon comes to illustrate his method of induction with his 'First Vintage' example, he does indeed, as we have seen, begin the procedure of induction by Exclusion, or Rejection of Natures from the Form of Heat. Moreover, this section of the work has an introductory passage containing the following highly 'falsificationist' remark: 'For it is manifest from what has been said that any one contradictory instance overthrows a conjecture as to the Form' (Bacon 1620: 321). In the context of his investigation into the 'Form of Heat', Bacon gives some further general accounts of his method of induction, in particular in the following two passages:

The first work therefore of true induction (as far as regards the discovery of Forms) is the rejection or exclusion of the several natures which are not found in some instance where the given nature is present, or are found in some instance where the given nature is absent, or are found to increase in some instance when the given nature decreases, or to decrease when the given nature increases. Then indeed after the rejection and exclusion has been duly made, there will remain at the bottom, all light opinions vanishing into smoke, a Form affirmative, solid and true and well defined. This is quickly said; but the way to come at it is winding and intricate. (Bacon 1620: 320)

In the process of exclusion are laid the foundations of true Induction, which however is not completed till it arrives at an Affirmative. (Bacon 1620: 322)

Bacon appears to be arguing in these passages that the procedure of true induction can, in effect, be reduced to that of exclusion and rejection. The picture is something like this. Suppose we are invest-igating the 'Nature' or 'Form' of something. Bacon seems to pre-suppose that there are only a finite, and perhaps even rather limited, number of possibilities as to what this nature could be. If we go through these in turn, using our tables to exclude and reject any candidates which give the wrong predictions, we will be left at last with a single 'Form affirmative'—'all light opinions vanishing into smoke'. Thus, as he says in the plan of the work, 'a due process of exclusion and rejection' will 'lead to an inevitable conclusion'.

Of course, in his actual example of the 'Form of Heat', this did not happen. The process of exclusion and rejection left open quite a number of possibilities, and Bacon had to try 'the affirmative way' to get a result. However, as I indicated earlier, this seems to me an expedient which Bacon adopted reluctantly while still be-lieving that a more thorough analysis would lead to an inevitable conclusion using only the method of exclusion and rejection. This is perhaps the standard interpretation of Bacon's thinking on induc-tion, but it has been challenged in Urbach's important study of Bacon. Urbach argues that Bacon's use of 'the affirmative way' in the 'First Vintage' was 'not an eleventh-hour expedient forced on Bacon, throwing his philosophy into disarray, but was foreshad-owed and implied by his philosophy' (Urbach 1987: 184).[1]

Although I disagree with Urbach on this point, I very much endorse another aspect of his study of Bacon. Urbach lays emphasis on the similarities which exist between several of Bacon's ideas and Popper's, and, in an interesting part of his book, he demonstrates this by giving a series of parallel quotations from Bacon and Popper which are clearly seen to be making the same point (see Urbach 1987: 86–90). My comment on this is the following. What Bacon and Popper have in common is a shared emphasis on the need to try to refute our hypotheses. All Urbach's parallel quotations deal with one aspect or another of this general point of view. On other matters, however—for example, the role of human insight and crea-tivity in science, the desirability and possibility of a method of in-ductive inference from a large number of observations, and so on—Bacon and Popper hold very different views.

3.3. Bacon's Method has Only Recently Come to be Used

I began this chapter by pointing out that Popper's statement— 'Induction, i.e. inference based on many observations, is a myth. It is neither a psychological fact, nor a fact of ordinary life, nor one of scientific procedure' (1963: 53)—is clearly contradicted by machine-learning programs such as ID3 or GOLEM. Yet what Popper says here about scientific procedure contained a good deal of truth *at the time when it was written*—that is, in 1963. As we have seen, the first machine-learning programs to be used successfully in science were Buchanan and Feigenbaum's Meta-DENDRAL, and Michalski's INDUCE. However, these appeared in the late 1970s and early 1980s, i.e. more than fifteen years after the passage quoted from Popper was published. Moreover, as I will argue in this section, Baconian or mechanical induction, although advocated by Bacon in 1620, was used, either not at all, or hardly at all, in science until the rise of artificial intelligence and the emergence of the machine-learning programs just mentioned.

Popper is not the only philosopher to have denied that Baconian induction has played a part in scientific procedure. Similar views were expressed by Meyerson in his 1908 book Identity and Reality.[2] Meyerson writes:

Bacon believed that one could arrive at scientific discoveries by mechanical processes of induction, so to speak; he went to great lengths in elaborating detailed plans the use of which would leave little to be attributed 'to the penetration and vigour of minds', making them, on the contrary, 'all nearly equal'. . . . It is incontestable that certain rules stated by Bacon (such as, for example, those of concomitant variations) are useful in scientific reasoning. But his tables or schemes, one may boldly affirm, have never been employed in a constant manner by a scientist worthy of that name; at any rate, no scientific discovery, great or small, is due to their application. . . . Liebig, after having declared that between experiments in Bacon's sense and true scientific research 'there is the same relation as between the noise a child produces by striking on a drum and music', . . . shows that, on the contrary, it is the scientific imagination which plays the most important role in discoveries, and that experiment, like the calculus, only aids in the process of thought. (Meyerson 1908: 391)

(It is worth noting here the characteristic stress on scientific imagination, and resistance to Bacon's idea that a method might render all minds nearly the same. Meyerson's book, incidentally, was particularly admired by Einstein.)

I would support both Meyerson and Popper to the extent that I have not been able to find a convincing example of the use of Baconian or mechanical induction in science prior to the appearance of the first successful machine-learning programs in the late 1970s and early 1980s. I do not want to maintain this position dogmatically, since it is difficult to survey the whole history of science over many hundreds of years, and some Baconian example may come to light. The examples I considered in Chapter 1 were in fact chosen because they were the most Baconian I could produce. Yet both, as we saw, fell short of constituting genuinely mechanical induction. Kepler certainly made inferences from the many observations of Tycho Brahe, and used induction in that sense; but his induction involved human insight, creativity, and imagination, so that it cannot be considered induction in Bacon's sense. The discovery of the sulphonamide drugs, on the other hand, did involve the mechanical generation of a sequence of hypotheses, most of which were eliminated by 'exclusion and rejection'. But these hypotheses were generated, not from the observed data, but from a heuristic which guided the research. Thus the generation of the hypotheses was not, in this case, by means of induction in the proper sense of the word— i.e. inference from previously collected data. Bacon, moreover, had no idea of heuristic principles, or how they might be used in science. Other possible examples of induction from the history of science prior to the late 1970s seem to me to fall into one or other of these two categories, and so not to be Baconian induction in the full sense of the term.

A rather different kind of case, which might be considered to be an example of mechanical induction, is provided by mathematical statistics.[3] In estimation, regression, and similar techniques, values for parameters, or linear models are generated from the data by mathematical methods which can indeed be applied in a routine fashion. Is this an instance of mechanical induction in the manner of Bacon? I am inclined to answer 'no'. All these statistical techniques boil down to the estimation of parameters, and this seems to me a generalization of the familiar process of measurement to probabilistic hypotheses, rather than a genuinely Baconian induction. Certainly there is nothing analogous to Bacon's suggested procedure of generating a number of possibilities from the data and then eliminating some of them by 'exclusion and rejection'. However, once again I have no wish to be dogmatic on this point, and there is no reason to be so. The modern statistical methods of estimation and regression came into regular use in science only after they had been developed mathematically by Fisher in the 1920s. So, even if they are genuine examples of mechanical induction, they emerge at least 300 years after the *Novum Organum*. Thus Bacon advocated a method in 1620 which was not used by scientists until the present century, but is now being taken up and developed by the AI community. How are we to explain this remarkable time lag, combined with final vindication?

Of course, much of Bacon's writing has a prophetic character. He lived at a time when some technological inventions such as printing, gunpowder, and the compass were beginning to have a considerable impact on life; and when some advances were occurring in theoretical science as well. Generalizing from this rather slender evidence, Bacon predicted, quite correctly as it turned out, that science and technology could have a glorious future and bring to light all sorts of marvels. Given his enthusiasm for the use of machines and instruments, it was a natural step for Bacon to suggest that thought itself should be mechanized and so made more productive. He was not, however, able to offer any *physical* instrument for helping human thought, beyond pen and paper. His recommendation was only in the direction of more systematic procedures for drawing up tables, and son on. But such procedures, unaccompanied by any physical machine, did not have any advantage over the less systematic, more intuitive, ways of thinking which are undoubtedly more natural to human beings. It was thus only with the development of the computer that Bacon's mechanical methods for thinking were able to come into their own for the first time.

Although about three and a half centuries separate the *Novum Organum* from the invention of the silicon chip, Bacon's idea of mechanizing thought was by no means universally abandoned during all this time. On the contrary, many thinkers tried to develop it in different ways, usually in conjunction with plans to construct or improve calculating machines. Leibniz, Babbage, Jevons, and Turing all worked in this general line of research, which was perhaps naturally suggested by their social environment. Given the great success of machines in the physical sphere, why not try to extend their use into the area of mental activity? This line of thought constitutes an important part of the intellectual background to the emergence of the computer.[4]

It has taken a long time for Bacon's dream of having instruments to assist scientific thinking to be realized. However, now that computers and artificial intelligence are beginning to play a part in scientific procedure, it is predictable that they will transform the way in which science is done and lead to a whole host of remarkable and surprising discoveries. An analogy will help to illustrate what may lie in store. Before the year 1609 observations in science had been made exclusively with unaided human sense organs. In that year, Galileo for the first time used an instrument to make scientific observations—namely, the telescope to survey the heavens. His discoveries were truly remarkable. He was able to observe mountains on the moon, and could see at least ten times as many stars as had previously been known. He found that the Milky Way consisted of innumerable stars and discovered that the planet Jupiter had moons circling round it.

All this showed the enormous advantage of improving naked-eye observation by the use of an instrument. Soon other instruments, such as the microscope, were devised, and nowadays hardly any science is carried out which does not use instruments. The development of instruments to assist the human sense organs has changed the way in which science is done, and brought about a vast extension of human knowledge. Is it not reasonable to suppose, therefore, that the development of instruments to help the human mind—i.e. computers furnished with AI programs—will have a similar effect on science?

It is important to realize that scientific method is not something fixed and ahistorical. Rather, as Bacon says in a quotation which I have used as the epigraph of this book, 'the art of discovery may advance as discoveries advance' (1620: 301). Meyerson and Popper were not wrong when, writing before the 1970s, they denied that Baconian induction formed part of scientific procedure. What they said was true of science as it had been practised up to that time. However, just as earlier the use of instruments to assist observation altered the way in which science was done, so the current development of computers and artificial intelligence is also destined to change science, and in such a way that Baconian induction becomes a standard part of scientific procedure.

3.4. The Need for Background Knowledge

I will conclude the chapter by mentioning in this final section a point which definitely favours Popper and goes somewhat against Bacon. As we have seen, all the successful machine-learning programs make use of background knowledge K, which is coded into the program and plays an essential role in guiding the computer's induction. Indeed, computer inferences really take the form: from K&e infer h, rather than the form: from e infer h. The importance of background knowledge is very much in accordance with Popper's ideas. Indeed Popper wrote, in a passage which I have already quoted, 'the belief that we can start with pure observations alone, without anything in the nature of a theory, is absurd . . .' (1963: 46). On the other hand, Bacon does not seem to have realized the importance of background knowledge, or understood its heuristic role. At all events, he never mentions these topics. His view seems to have been that, in any investigation, there are only a finite number of possible hypotheses, and we can therefore reach the correct one in a straightforward manner by the exclusion and rejection of the others. The inadequacy of this view is shown by the drug-discovery case. It would scarcely be possible to test for therapeutic properties every single compound which the chemists of today are capable of synthesizing, since there are an indefinitely large number of such compounds. In this situation there has to be a recourse to heuristics. In the case of the discovery of the sulphonamide drugs, the 'dye heuristic' was used, and this, as we saw, was based on some findings of Ehrlich which were well known to Domagk and his team. In general it seems to be possible to identify heuristics with background knowledge (or assumptions), and the background knowledge coded into machine-learning programs has a heuristic role. Thus ID3 requires a set of concepts suitable for describing the domain in question. Nine-place predicates were coded into GOLEM's background knowledge in the protein-folding problem, and this guided the program to look for laws determining the character of a residue in terms of the four residues on each side of it. Many further instances could be given from the examples considered in Chapter 2.

The importance of background knowledge will be a key argument for the analysis which I will present in Chapter 6 of how humans and computers may interact in the new scientific procedures which are even now emerging. The main point I will make there is that it is a mistake to think of computers replacing human scientists. The model should rather be one of human–machine interaction. Human knowledge is coded into the computer, but then the computer comes up with new results which give human scientists plenty of scope for further thought and reflection, and so on. This interactive process should give humans greater powers for making scientific discoveries than before, and provide more, not less, scope for human intuitive thought with its capacity for insight and creativity.

This, however, is a theme for Chapter 6. In the next chapter I will temporarily leave the topic of induction, and consider instead the advances that have been made in logic programming, and the implications these have for the foundations of logic. Then, in Chapter 5, I will combine the discussions of Chapters 1–3 and Chapter 4 by considering what light our investigations can shed on an old question in philosophy of science—the question of whether there can be an inductive logic, and, if so, what form such a logic should take.

4 Logic Programming and a New Framework for Logic

THE aim of this chapter is to explore some consequences for the philosophy of logic of the development of the logic programming system PROLOG. These consequences, it will be argued, are of considerable importance. Although PROLOG developed from studies of classical predicate logic, it led to a new kind of logic, so-called non-monotonic logic. The logic of PROLOG is very far from being the first non-classical logic, but it is the first non-classical logic which has proved to be useful in some practical applications. This situation, as I will argue, strengthens the view that logic is empirical rather than *a priori*. PROLOG, moreover, introduces control into deductive logic and thus suggests a new framework in which logic is thought of, not merely as inference, but as inference + *control*. This framework will prove valuable in the next chapter, in which we shall consider the question of whether there can be an inductive logic, and, if so, what form that logic should take.

In the first section of this chapter (4.1) I will give a brief account of how PROLOG was developed,[1] and then in the subsequent sections of the chapter I will explore the various philosophical implications of PROLOG just described.

4.1. The Development of PROLOG

PROLOG arose when two different fields of investigation were brought together. Historians of science and mathematics have noted that this is a not uncommon pattern of advance. For example, Grosholz (1992) argues that significant, sudden increases of knowledge can result from the bringing-together of previously unrelated domains. She illustrates this thesis by the example of Leibniz, who, she argues, came to the calculus through his synthesis of geometry, algebra, and number theory, and then further extended it by connecting these areas to mechanics as well.

In the case of PROLOG, one of the two different lines of investigation was automated theorem-proving. Here the seminal paper was Robinson's (1965), which, as we have seen, also exercised an influence on the development of the machine-learning program GOLEM. Robinson set himself the task of developing a form of ordinary classical 1st-order logic which would be suitable for theorem-proving on the computer. Building on Herbrand's work, he formulated the clausal form of logic with a single rule of inference (*the resolution principle*). He showed that this system was complete, and equivalent to 1st-order classical logic. He pointed out that the direct implementation of the proof of completeness would yield a proof-procedure for the computer, but that this would be quite inefficient. He accordingly concluded his paper with a discussion of several search principles which could improve the efficiency of proof-procedures employing the resolution principle. These investigations were continued, and significant results obtained in Loveland (1969), Kowalski and Kuehner (1971), and Reiter (1971).

The second line of investigation was into natural language processing. Alain Colmerauer headed an AI group in Marseilles who were trying to develop a natural language question-answering system. The group included Robert Pasero and Philippe Roussel. Roussel had read Kowalski and Kuehner (1971) and thought that the SL-resolution theorem-prover developed there might be used for the deductive component of the question-answering system. (SL-resolution is short for linear resolution with a selection function.) Accordingly, Colmerauer invited Kowalski, then at Edinburgh, to visit the Marseilles group for a few days in the summer of 1971.

Colmerauer and Kowalski were not only working on different problems, but were also different in temperament and outlook. Colmerauer combined his theoretical interests in computer science with close attention to the practical side, and to implementations. Kowalski describes himself as 'a logician at heart, who suffered a faint revulsion for programming and everything else to do with computers' (1988: 39). Despite, or perhaps because of, these differences, the two men got on very well, and had long discussions about using logic to represent grammar and using resolution to parse sentences. They also planned to meet again soon, and in fact Kowalski returned to Marseilles, again at Colmerauer's invitation, in the spring of 1972. In the discussions of that spring the idea of programming in predicate logic was born. The subsequent actions of Colmerauer and Kowalski were characteristic of the temperamental differences already noted.

In the summer of 1972 Colmerauer and Roussel designed and implemented the first PROLOG system in ALGOL-W as an adaptation of Roussel's existing SL-resolution theorem-prover. Then with other members of the team they implemented a large natural language processing system. This was the first major program in PROLOG. It was written in 1972, and described in Colmerauer, Kanoui, Pasero, and Roussel (1973). The name PROLOG was suggested by Roussel's wife, Jacqueline, as an abbreviation for *programmation en logique*.

Kowalski meanwhile wrote a theoretical paper on predicate logic as a programming language, later published in revised form (Kowalski 1974) Here he introduced the *procedural interpretation* of Horn clause logic. Another important theoretical contribution was made by Boyer and Moore at Edinburgh, who argued (1972) that certain ways of efficiently implementing theorem-provers resemble ways of implementing programming language interpreters. This suggested that theorem-provers could be regarded as interpreters for programs written in predicate logic. Running through all these developments is the idea of synthesizing logic as a procedure (deduction, theorem-proving, etc.), with logic as a language.

In his 1988 memoir Kowalski states with considerable frankness that, although he was very enthusiastic about the use of predicate logic as a programming language, he was not initially very impressed by the practical implementation of the Marseilles group. His doubts arose because PROLOG used only very simple heuristic and search strategies, whereas Kowalski was investigating more sophisticated and varied strategies, some of which are described in his book (1979b). Kowalski writes: 'It was not until around 1976 when I was at Imperial College in London that I finally appreciated the ingenious, delicate balance that Prolog achieved between being a fairly primitive, but useful, theorem prover, and being a very high-level programming language' (1988: 40).

It will be obvious by now that many different strands of thought enter into PROLOG, and in the remainder of this chapter I will try to separate out some of these and discuss their significance. Before closing this section, however, two further important contributions must be mentioned.

In his 1973 paper, Hayes stressed the importance of *control*, and this idea was taken up and developed by Kowalski in 'Algorithm Equals Logic Plus Control' (1979*a*). This introduction of control into logic seems to me a step of crucial importance, and I will discuss it in detail in Sections 4.4. and 4.5.

The earlier theoretical work of Robinson, Loveland, Kowalski and Kuehner, and Reiter had all been concerned with the problem of adapting ordinary classical 1st-order logic for the computer. In the course of actually implementing PROLOG, it turned out that use had to be not of classical negation, but of a different type of negation called *negation-as-failure*. This issue was clarified by Clark (1978), which contains a study of this new type of negation. Although negation-as-failure was one of the last elements of PROLOG to be studied, it turns out to be the most convenient starting-point for our own investigation of the philosophical implications of PROLOG. I will therefore consider it in detail in the next section (4.2)

4.2. PROLOG as a Non-Monotonic Logic: Negation-as-Failure and the Closed World Assumption

In this section I will argue that PROLOG is based not on standard classical logic, but on what is known as non-monotonic logic. To explain the non-monotonic character of PROLOG it will be helpful to consider an example. Now PROLOG is of great practical use in dealing with travel problems concerned with timetables and routes. Indeed PROLOG was the basis of an actual travel-planning program used by the travel agents Thomas Cook for arranging routes on the Australian railway network. Regrettably I have never been to Australia, but it seems that using the Australian railway network is no simple matter. Suppose, for example, you want to travel from Alice Springs to Perth. On the map it looks as if the right place to change would be Tarcoola, but no expert on Australian railways would recommend this strategy. It seems that trains from Alice Springs, which have to cover many hundreds of miles of desert, are often delayed by sand storms or even flash floods. Thus changing at Tarcoola could easily result in missing a connection, and having to spend two days waiting in Tarcoola for the next train. Those who know Tarcoola maintain that this would not be a pleasant experience, even for the leisurely traveller. Now the full Thomas Cook program incorporates expert knowledge of this kind, and is therefore somewhat complicated. However, to illustrate the logical character of PROLOG, it suffices to consider a much simpler travel problem.

Suppose that I have to give a lecture at 10 a.m. on a Monday morning. I therefore look in a timetable for the trains from North Dulwich to London Bridge on a Monday morning. I find that there are trains at 7 a.m., 8 a.m., 9 a.m., and 10 a.m. (This may seem rather few trains, but we can suppose that the government has cut back services in the run-up to privatization.) In the normal course of events I would simply select the appropriate train, and computers would not enter the picture. Suppose, however, for the sake of illustration, that, instead of possessing a timetable, I have the data on train times stored in a PROLOG logic program in my PC at home. Let us first see a simple way in which the information might be coded.

Let p(X). = def A train leaves North Dulwich for London Bridge at X a.m. on Monday morning.

Note that in PROLOG with the usual Edinburgh-Syntax any term starting with a capital letter denotes a variable, while any term starting with a lower-case letter denotes a constant. Thus a specific propositional function is denoted by $p(X)$ rather than the customary $P(x)$.

Using the above notation, we can suppose that the timetable information has been stored in my computer as follows:

p(7).
p(8).
p(9).
p(10).

This is a well-defined PROLOG logic program, which we can call dultimetable.1.

Let us now see how I might consult this logic program. Let us suppose that it takes me about one hour from catching a train at North Dulwich to arriving in College. I am lecturing at 10 a.m. So it would be convenient to arrive at 9.30 a.m. I would, therefore, like to catch a train from North Dulwich at 8.30 a.m., if there is one. I therefore interact with the computer as follows:

?- p(8.30).
no

Here I type in the first line, and the computer answers by producing 'no'. PROLOG has inferred not p(8.30) from the database. However, this inference is not valid according to classical logic. The database merely says that there are trains at 7 a.m., 8 a.m., 9 a.m., and 10 a.m. It does not follow from this by standard logic that there is not a train also at 8.30 a.m. There may be such a train which has not been listed in the database.

To obtain not p(8.30), PROLOG has used, instead of classical negation, what is called negation-as-failure. This works as follows. PROLOG tries to prove p(8.30) by attempting to match this sentence against the sentences in the database. When it fails to prove p(8.30), it concludes not p(8.30)—i.e. it uses negation-as-failure. This use of negation-as-failure turns PROLOG into what is called a 'non-monotonic' logic. I will next explain what this means.

Suppose that in classical logic, a proposition p follows logically from a set of premisses Γ, or in symbols $\Gamma \vdash p$. Let Δ be an arbitrary set of further premisses, then p still follows logically from the union of Γ with Δ, i.e. $\Gamma \cup \Delta \vdash p$. To see that this is so, suppose that p does not follow logically from $\Gamma \cup \Delta$. There is then an interpretation in which p is false, but all the propositions in $\Gamma \cup \Delta$ are true. In this interpretation p is false, and all the propositions in Γ are true, and so p does not follow logically from Γ either. In classical logic then, if a conclusion follows from some premisses, it still follows however many additional premisses we add to our original set of premisses. This is why classical logic is called monotonic. The set of conclusions increases monotonically as we add more premisses.

PROLOG with negation-as-failure is not, however, monotonic. If I add to the database dultimetable.1 an additional proposition p(8.30), the conclusion not p(8.30) no longer follows as it did before. Instead PROLOG will infer p(8.30). So the logic of PROLOG is not ordinary classical logic, but a particular kind of non-monotonic logic.[2]

Someone might object that I am really exaggerating the difference between the logic of PROLOG and classical logic. The logic of PROLOG, it might be argued, is really just classical logic with an unstated, but implicit, premiss. In the case of dultimetable.1, this implicit premiss is that the trains explicitly listed are all the trains from North Dulwich to London Bridge on a Monday morning. This premiss is sometimes called the closed world assumption, or CWA. The world in question is that of trains from North Dulwich to London Bridge on a Monday morning. CWA claims that this is a closed world consisting of just those trains explicitly listed in the database by different substitutions for X in the propositional function p(X). If we now add p(8.30) to dultimetable.1, CWA could still be formulated in the same words, but it would now have a different meaning. Our implicit premiss would have changed, and this explains why, remaining fully in accord with classical logic, we can now draw different conclusions.

The trouble with this approach is that PROLOG with negation-as-failure is not in fact equivalent to classical logic with CWA. This is shown by the following example.[3] Suppose that there is a by-law which says that, if there is no 7.30 a.m. train from North Dulwich to London Bridge on a Monday morning, there will be a 8.30 a.m. train. In PROLOG, using Edinburgh-Syntax, this would be written: p(8.30) :- not p(7.30), which can be read as: 'p(8.30), if not p(7.30)'. Let us therefore add: 'p(8.30) :- not p(7.30).' to the sentences of dultimetable.1 to obtain a new logic program dultimetable.2. We will now examine how CWA, and negation-as-failure, work for dultimetable.2.

Our query is whether there is a train at 8.30 a.m. from North Dulwich to London Bridge on a Monday morning—i.e. ?- p(8.30). If we accept CWA, as formulated above, and classical logic then the answer is 'no', because p(8.30) is not explicitly listed in dultimetable.2. PROLOG, however, produces the following interaction:

?- p(8.30).
yes

On being given the query, PROLOG tries to prove p(8.30). It matches p(8.30), to the left-hand side of the sentence p(8.30) :- not p(7.30), and concludes that it can prove p(8.30), if it can prove not p(7.30). It therefore tries to prove not p(7.30). Now p(7.30) cannot be matched to anything in the logic program dultimetable.2, and so the attempt to prove p(7.30) fails. Thus by negation-as-failure, not p(7.30) is proved, and so p(8.30) is proved. This shows that classical logic with CWA can give different results from PROLOG with negation-as-failure.

This is not, however, the end of the argument, because I have stated the closed world assumption in a particularly simple fashion. It could be objected that, by formulating CWA in a more complicated fashion, it might still be possible to show that classical logic with CWA is equivalent to PROLOG with negation-as-failure. Since there is no limit to the ingenuity of mathematicians, I am perfectly prepared to admit that this might indeed be possible. Gabbay has shown recently (1993) that a whole group of non-classical logics can be translated into classical logic, but this does not show, in my opinion, that these non-classical logics are 'really' classical logic in disguise. That would be like saying that, because Jane Austen's novels can be translated into French, they are 'really' part of French literature. Rather than take the logic of a system to be 'really' something else obtainable by hypothetical implicit assumptions and complicated translations, it seems to me more natural to identify the logic with what is clearly and explicitly set out and applied in practice. This, in general terms, is my argument for regarding the logic of PROLOG as non-monotonic rather than classical. I believe that this argument can be strengthened by examining some well-known translations which exist between logical systems and, in particular, one of Gödel's translations of classical into intuitionistic logic.[4] I will consider these translations in the next section, which consequently presupposes some knowledge of both classical and intuitionistic logic. Readers unfamiliar with these topics can, without losing the main thread of the argument, move on to Section 4.4, which introduces the new subject of control.

*4.3. Two Examples of Translations from One Logical System to Another

Let us suppose, for the sake of argument, that there is a successful translation of PROLOG with negation-as-failure into classical logic, obtained by formulating a stronger version of CWA as an 'implicit assumption', or in some other way. As a matter of fact, no such translation has, to my knowledge, been set out explicitly and in detail, but, at the same time, it is by no means implausible that such a translation might be found. It is therefore worth raising the question of whether such a translation would show that PROLOG is really just classical logic after all and not a new non-monotonic logic. My aim is to argue that such a conclusion could not be drawn from the existence of a successful translation. The argument is from a consideration of the translations invented by Gödel from classical into intuitionistic logic. These translations (see Gödel 1933, or Heyting 1956: 7.3.3, pp. 112–13) are indeed successful, but they do not show that classical logic is really intuitionistic logic. Similarly a successful translation of PROLOG into classical logic would not show that PROLOG is really classical rather than non-monotonic logic. I will consider one of Gödel's translations in a moment, but it will be useful to give first an example of a much simpler translation which does indeed show two logical systems to be equivalent. This case can then conveniently be compared with the more complicated Gödel case.

Let us consider then an axiomatic formulation of the propositional calculus which uses only the connectives ~ (not), ⊃ (implies) ($\mathbf{P}_1$, say), and another axiomatic formulation which uses only the connectives ~ (not), & (and) ($\mathbf{P}_2$, say). Let us introduce the translation according to which

~p	goes into	~p
p ⊃ q	goes into	~(p & ~q)

In this translation, all the theorems of $\mathbf{P}_1$ translate into theorems of $\mathbf{P}_2$. Conversely, let us introduce the translation according to which

~p	goes into	~p
p & q	goes into	~(p ⊃ ~q)

In this translation, all the theorems of $\mathbf{P}_2$ translate into theorems of $\mathbf{P}_1$. Now most people would agree that these translations do establish that $\mathbf{P}_1$ and $\mathbf{P}_2$ are equivalent, and are just two different formulations of the same logic—namely, classical propositional calculus. The point of introducing this very elementary example is to contrast this situation with that obtaining in the case of translations between classical and intuitionistic logic. Although such translations do exist, I want to argue that they do not establish that classical and intuitionistic logic are really the same logic. It will therefore be necessary to examine why the classical/intuitionistic case differs from the elementary case just considered. It will help us to bring out the differences involved, if, before introducing one of the Gödel translations, I make a number of points about intuitionistic logic. It will suffice to consider intuitionistic propositional calculus, and I will base my account on Heyting's (1956) exposition.

As the preceding example implied, an axiomatic formulation of classical propositional calculus can be based on only two connectives. Heyting, however, in his axiomatic formulation of intuitionistic propositional calculus uses four connectives: ∧ (and), v (or), ¬ (not), → (implies). It will be convenient to use different signs for the classical analogues of these four connectives, namely: & (and), or (or), ~ (not), ⊃ (implies). I will argue that the classical connectives have a different meaning from the intuitionistic ones, so that a different sign is quite appropriate.

Let us begin with negation (not). The classical connective ∼, like all the classical connectives, is defined using the concepts of true and false. Thus ∼p is true if p is false, and false if p is true. Intuitionistic negation ¬ is defined in quite a different way. Heyting explains the concept roughly as follows:

Strictly speaking, we must well distinguish the use of 'not' in mathematics from that in explanations which are not mathematical, but are expressed in ordinary language. In mathematical assertions no ambiguity can arise: 'not' has always the strict meaning. 'The proposition p is not true', or 'the proposition p is false' means 'If we suppose the truth of p, we are led to a contradiction'. (Heyting 1956: 18)

Intuitionistic negation is, of course, the strict or mathematical meaning of 'not'. Heyting's explanation is, however, a little imprecise. ¬ p does indeed mean that the assumption of p can be shown to lead to a contradiction, but we should really say 'can be shown *constructively* to lead to a contradiction', because intuitionism is concerned with constructive mathematics. Heyting makes this clear in a later passage where he explains the meaning of all the four intuitionistic connectives. The passage runs as follows:

The *conjunction* ∧ gives no difficulty. **p** ∧ **q**[5] can be asserted if and only if both **p** and **q** can be asserted.

I have already spoken of the disjunction v . . . **p** v **q** can be asserted if and only if at least one of the propositions **p** and **q** can be asserted.

The negation ¬ is the strong mathematical negation which we have already discussed (2.2.2). In order to give a more explicit clarification, we remember that a mathematical proposition **p** always demands a mathematical construction with certain given properties; it can be asserted as soon as such a construction has been carried out. We say in this case that the construction *proves* the proposition **p** and call it a *proof* of **p**. We also, for the sake of brevity, denote by **p** any construction which is intended by the proposition **p**. Then ¬ **p** can be asserted if and only if we possess a construction which from the supposition that a construction **p** were carried out, leads to a contradiction. . . .

The *implication* **p** → **q** can be asserted, if and only if we possess a construction **r**, which, joined to any construction proving **p** (supposing the latter be effected), would automatically effect a construction proving **q**. In other words, a proof of **p**, together with **r**, would form a proof of **q**. (Heyting 1956: 98–9)

A general point worth noting is that the meaning of the intuitionistic connectives is explained in terms of the conditions under which it is legitimate to *assert* propositions. Thus, if ∗ is a typical connective, the meaning of **p** * **q** would be explained by saying when we can assert this composite proposition, in terms perhaps of the conditions when **p** and **q** can themselves be asserted, and/or in terms of when certain constructions can be produced. By contrast, the classical connectives are explained using the concepts of true and false. Thus if * were a classical rather than intuitionistic connective, the meaning of **p** * **q** would be explained by saying which truth values of the component propositions **p** and **q** make the composite proposition true and which make it false. The intuitionistic theory of meaning is based on *assertibility conditions*, while the classical theory of meaning is based on *truth conditions*, as Dummett has stressed in his writings on the subject (see Dummett 1973, 1977).

Let us next look in more detail at intuitionistic negation. In the second passage quoted, Heyting clarifies that $\neg$ p can be asserted if we possess a construction which shows that the assertion of p leads to a contradiction. Thus intuitionistic negation, like negation-as-failure, differs from classical negation, though the differences are not the same in the two cases. The different sense of intuitionistic negation shows up in the fact that it obeys different laws from classical negation. Thus, in classical propositional calculus, both $p \supset \sim\sim p$ and $\sim\sim p \supset p$ are theorems (tautologies). Indeed, it is obvious from the definition of classical negation that p and $\sim\sim p$ must be equivalent in truth value. In intuitionistic propositional calculus, $p \rightarrow \neg\neg p$ continues to hold, but $\neg\neg p \rightarrow p$ (the law of double negation) is no longer universally valid. It is worth presenting a counter-example to the law of double negation, as this will help to give a feel for intuitionistic logic. This counter-example is taken from Heyting (1956: 17–18).

Define a number ρ as follows. $\rho = 0.333 \ldots$ where we stop at the nth place if and only if $0123 \ldots 9$ are the n+1, n+2, ..., n+10th digits in the decimal expansion of π. Let p be the proposition: 'ρ is rational'. Then we can show intuitionistically that $\neg \neg$ p. For, if $\neg$ p, it is absurd to suppose we can construct integers k,l such that $\rho = k/l$. Hence it is absurd to suppose that $0123 \ldots 9$ occurs in the decimal expansion at the n+1, n+2, ..., n+10th places. For if it did, then

$$\rho = \frac{33 \ldots 3}{100 \ldots 0}, \text{ where there are n 3's above, and n 0's below}$$

giving us the values for k,l. So we can conclude, given $\neg$ p, that $0123 \ldots 9$ does not occur in the decimal expansion of π. But then

$\rho = \frac{1}{3}$, and so ρ is rational, i.e. p. This is a contradiction. Therefore $\neg \neg$ p holds. However, we cannot assert p i.e. ρ is rational, because this could be done only if we could construct integers k,l such that $\rho = k/l$.

The difference in their concepts of negation is one of the principal differences between classical and intuitionistic logic. However, there are differences even in some formulas which do not involve negation. Thus, $(p \supset q)$ or $(q \supset p)$ is a theorem (tautology) of classical logic, but $(p \rightarrow q)$ v $(q \rightarrow p)$ does not hold in intuitionistic logic. Really all the intuitionistic connectives differ from their classical counterparts because they are defined in terms of assertibility conditions rather than truth conditions. The most famous logical law which holds classically but fails intuitionistically is, of course, the law of the excluded middle. In its classical form (p or ~p) it is a theorem (tautology) of the classical propositional calculus, but the intuitionistic form p v $\neg$ p does not hold in the intuitionistic propositional calculus.

Heyting (1956: 7.1.3, pp. 101–2) presents an axiomatic formulation of intuitionistic propositional calculus, which he first published in 1930. The axioms and rules of inference are all classically valid when one replaces the intuitionistic by classical connectives. However, not all classically valid results are derivable in the system. For example, it is not possible to derive the law of double negation, or the law of excluded middle. Intuitionistic logic thus appears as a subset of classical logic—a narrower, but perhaps more certain system. It therefore came as a surprise when, three years after Heyting published his axiomatization, Gödel was able to show that it is possible to translate the whole of classical logic into a subset of intuitionistic logic. I will now give Gödel's translations for the propositional calculus. They are as follows:

p or q	goes into	$\neg \, (\neg \, p \wedge \neg \, q)$
p & q	goes into	$p \wedge q$
p $\supset$ q	goes into	$\neg \, (p \wedge \neg \, q)$
~p	goes into	$\neg \, p$

With these translations, every tautology of the classical propositional calculus is transformed into a theorem of the intuitionistic propositional calculus. In particular, every ordinary tautology expressed using only the connectives 'and' and 'not' remains valid intuitionistically if 'and' and 'not' are given their intuitionistic meaning.

Now does this translation establish that classical logic is 'really' intuitionistic logic? It seems to me obvious that it does not. The translation transforms any classical theorem (T, say) into an intuitionistic theorem (T', say), but T' *does not have the same meaning as* T, because the translation *does not preserve the meaning of the connectives*. This can be seen most easily in the case of the connectives 'and' and 'not'. The classical & is translated by the intuitionistic ∧, and the classical ~ by the intuitionistic ¬ . However, as we have pointed out in detail in our account of intuitionistic logic, the classical connectives &, ~ simply do not have the same meanings as the intuitionistic connectives ∧, ¬ . The classical connectives are defined by truth conditions, while the intuitionistic connectives are defined by assertibility conditions of quite a different character. The point can be seen more clearly by comparing the Gödel translation with the simple translations which showed the equivalence of the two axiomatic formulations of classical propositional calculus P_1 and P_2. The translation of P_1 into P_2 was the following:

~p   goes into   ~p
p ⊃ q   goes into   ~(p & ~q)

It is clear that this translation does preserve the meaning of the connectives. ~ goes into itself. As for ⊃, we are in the classical framework, so that all the connectives are defined by truth conditions. It is thus a simple exercise in truth tables to show that the translation of ⊃ preserves its usual meaning.

Generalizing from this, let us distinguish two different types of translation of one logical system (L, say) into another (M, say). A *formally correct* translation is one which maps any theorem (or valid formula) of L into a theorem (or valid formula) of M. An *adequate* translation is a formally correct translation which preserves the meaning of the key terms. Now translations can be formally correct without being adequate, and we need to have an adequate translation in order to say that L does not express a different logical system from M, and that L is shown to be part of the logical system expressed by M.

The analogy of Gödel's translations of classical into intuitionistic logic suggests that any translation of PROLOG into classical logic will be formally correct without being adequate. Of course, since such a translation is hypothetical rather than explicitly worked out, this is a plausible rather than a decisive argument. However, it should be remembered that PROLOG, like intuitionistic logic, has a form of negation which is clearly distinct from classical negation. It is unlikely that any translation into classical logic will preserve the meaning of negation-as-failure. Moreover, PROLOG does not differ from classical logic only because of negation-as-failure. There is a further and more profound difference, which is concerned with the question of *control*. Indeed, as we shall see, negation-as-failure itself arises out of considerations about control. I will introduce the concept of control in the next section (4.4), and then explore its implications for the philosophy of logic in Section 4.5.

4.4. Logic = Inference + Control

When developing his ideas about logic programming, Kowalski introduced the formula (which has subsequently become famous):

$$\text{Algorithm} = \text{Logic} + \text{Control} \qquad (A = L + C)$$

As he himself says: 'Logic programs express only the *logic component* L of algorithms. The *control component* C is exercised by the program executor, either following its own autonomously determined control decisions or else following control instructions provided by the programmer' (Kowalski 1979b: 125).

I next want to propose a kind of extension of Kowalski's formula which I think will provide a useful framework for the discussions which follow. The new formula is

$$\text{Logic} = \text{Inference} + \text{Control} \qquad (L = I + C)$$

The picture is this. When we employ Logic, we start with a set of assumptions from which we want to derive some conclusions. To carry out these derivations we need a set of rules of inference (the Inference component). However, in addition to these rules of inference, we will generally also need in practice some guidance as to which assumptions to choose and which rules of inference to apply. This guidance constitutes the Control component. Thus the Control component might specify, at each stage of the derivation, which of the assumptions we should employ, and which of the rules of inference should be applied to these assumptions or to previously obtained results. More generally, the Control component would be designed to help in the construction of a derivation or proof of a conclusion.

The formula Logic = Inference + Control has strong links with

Gabbay's conception of a Labelled Deductive System (see Gabbay 1991). In Gabbay's approach, each formula of the logic is labelled, and the rules of inference are augmented with rules of manipulation for the labels. The labels and the rules for their manipulation can often be considered as a way of expressing the Control component.

4.5. PROLOG Introduces Control into Deductive Logic

There is an interesting contrast between the study of quantum logic and the development of PROLOG. The proponents of quantum logic deliberately suggested changing classical logic in order to resolve some of the problems of quantum mechanics. I think it fair to say that this attempt proved to be a failure. A change of logic did not, as it turned out, help to resolve the conceptual difficulties of quantum mechanics. By contrast, those who developed logic programming had no intention of changing logic. They merely wanted to apply the already existing, and well-established, systems of logic to a new problem—that of computer programming. However, by adapting classical logic for the computer, they inadvertently changed it. Thus the quantum logicians were conscious revolutionaries who failed to carry out their revolution. The logic programmers, who had no revolutionary intentions, none the less started a revolution in logic.

We have already argued that PROLOG, because of its negation-as-failure, turned out to be a non-monotonic logic. We must next examine what is really a much more profound change—namely, PROLOG's introduction of control into deductive logic.[6] This can be illustrated by an analogy. The development of PROLOG (and indeed of formal logic in general) can be seen as a process of replacing *craft skill* by *mechanization*. It is thus analogous to the change from hand-loom weaving to weaving with the power loom, and similar industrial transformations.

In terms of this analogy, the Fregean revolution in logic (1879–c.1931) can be seen as the mechanization of the process of checking a mathematical proof for validity. Before this revolution (and indeed for long after up to the present day), mathematical proofs were written out informally using natural language as well as symbolism. To check whether a proposed proof was indeed valid was no easy task and had to be carried out by a trained mathematician, one of whose 'craft skills' was that of checking whether a given line in a proof followed logically from what had gone before. Often disagreements occurred as to whether a proof was valid—though usually they were resolved after some discussion. Once a proof is written out in a formal language with all the logical steps fully explicit, the checking of the proof ceases to be a craft skill and becomes a purely mechanical task which can be carried out by a computer.

It is interesting to note that Frege at times comes close to the above conception of what he is doing. Thus he writes in the preface to his *Begriffsschrift*:

To prevent anything intuitive [*Anschauliches*] from penetrating here unnoticed, I had to bend every effort to keep the chain of inferences free of gaps. In attempting to comply with this requirement in the strictest possible way I found the inadequacy of language to be an obstacle; no matter how unwieldy the expressions I was ready to accept, I was less and less able, as the relations became more and more complex, to attain the precision that my purpose required. This deficiency led me to the idea of the present ideography. Its first purpose, therefore, is to provide us with the most reliable test of the validity of a chain of inferences and to point out every presupposition that tries to sneak in unnoticed, so that its origin can be investigated. (Frege 1879: 5–6)

Frege aims to eliminate 'anything intuitive' from his proofs. He must here be referring to the intuitions of trained mathematicians, and these are part of what we have called their 'craft skills'. To achieve this elimination of intuition, Frege tries 'to keep the chain of inferences free of gaps'. He finds it necessary to translate the expressions into a special formal language invented for the purpose (his *Begriffsschrift*—literally, 'concept writing'), and he sees this procedure as providing us 'with the most reliable test of the validity of a chain of inferences'.

While Frege's work showed an implicit tendency towards a mechanization of logic, Jevons had earlier explicitly adopted the plan of mechanizing logic. Indeed, Jevons actually had a logical machine constructed by a clockmaker in 1869, and gives a description of it in his work of 1870, which, significantly, is entitled 'On the Mechanical Performance of Logical Inference'. This device, known as 'Jevons's logical piano', does actually resemble a piano in appearance. By pressing the keys, an operator can input premises and cause a logical inference to be drawn mechanically. A picture of the logical piano appears as an illustration at the beginning of Jevons's (1874) *The Principles of Science*. This is one of the few contemporary works cited by Frege. Frege refers to an English edition of it on many occasions in his *Foundations of Arithmetic* (1884: e.g. sect. 16, p. 22). Moreover, Frege explicitly mentions Jevons's logical machine in a manuscript entitled 'Boole's Logical Calculus and the Concept-Script', which Frege wrote in 1880–1 but which was printed only after his death because it was rejected by the editors of the three journals to which Frege submitted it. Frege writes: 'Boole presupposes logically perfect concepts as ready to hand . . . he can then draw his inferences from the given assumptions by a mechanical process of computation. Stanley Jevons has in fact invented a machine to do this' (1880–1: 34–5). However, Frege goes on to stress that this mechanization covers only a part of human thinking: 'Boolean formula-language only represents a part of our thinking; our thinking as a whole can never be coped with by a machine or replaced by purely mechanical activity' (1880–1: 35). This accords with our analysis of Frege as mechanizing only one part of logic (the checking of proofs), while Jevons, with his logical machine, anticipates the further mechanization of logic to be found in PROLOG.[7]

Classical (and indeed intuitionistic) logic can then be seen as mechanizing the process of checking the validity of a proof, while leaving the construction of the proof entirely in the hands of the human mathematician, who has to use his or her craft skills to carry out the task. PROLOG carries the mechanization process one stage further by mechanizing the construction of proofs. In this respect, then, it goes beyond classical logic.

Suppose we have a PROLOG database (including programs). If the user inputs a query—e.g. ?- p(a). (i.e. is p(a) true?)—PROLOG will automatically try to construct a proof of p(a) from the database. If it succeeds in proving p(a), the answer will be 'yes', while, if it fails to prove p(a), the answer will be 'no'. In order to construct these proofs, PROLOG contains a set of instructions (often called the PROLOG interpreter) for searching systematically through various possibilities. The method is *depth first, left-to-right* search. This means that the leftmost branch of the search space is explored until the tip of the tree is reached. The exploration then continues from left to right in the hope of finding a solution. If this leads to failure, *backtracking* occurs to a point, specified by the interpreter, from which the search starts again. The instructions for carrying out such searches are clearly part of a control system which has been added to the inference procedures of classical logic.

PROLOG is often referred to as a logic programming language. Thus, in their admirable textbook, Mueller and Page say: 'We have occasionally alluded to Prolog as a *logic programming* language' (1988: ch. 33, p. 291). Now this turn of phrase has certainly something to commend it. The sentences of PROLOG are written in a language which is a variant of the language of the predicate calculus standardly used by logicians. Thus the sentence of ordinary language: 'All swans are white' would be written: '$(\forall x)(\text{swan}(x) \rightarrow \text{white}(x))$' in predicate calculus, while in PROLOG, using Edinburgh-Syntax, it appears as: white(X) :- swan(X). The PROLOG sentence can be read as: 'X is white, if X is a swan'. However, to speak of PROLOG as a logic programming language is misleading if it suggests that PROLOG is just a formal language. In fact, PROLOG is more than just a language, and can be more correctly considered as a *system of logic*. This system contains not just a formal language, but also rules of inference, and an elaborate control mechanism designed to carry out searches and construct proofs. This situation means that PROLOG sentences have, in addition to their *declarative* interpretation, a *procedural* interpretation of the kind described by Kowalski (1974). Consider again: white(X) :- swan(X). The declarative interpretation is that all swans are white. The procedural interpretation is that, if you want to establish the goal of showing that X is white, you can try to establish the subgoal of showing that X is a swan. This is precisely the way in which the PROLOG interpreter makes use of the rule: white(X) :- swan(X).

Let us now consider those differences between PROLOG and classical logic which arise from the fact that PROLOG contains an elaborate control mechanism designed to conduct searches and construct proofs.[8] Mueller and Page (1988: 292) define a *logic program* as 'a conjunction . . . of a finite set of Horn *clauses* . . .'. Once again, although this definition is not exactly wrong, it could be misleading, because it does not mention the essential element of control which is needed to make logic programs work. Often, of course, the control is exercised by the PROLOG interpreter, and so does not appear in the logic program itself, but sometimes the control element is explicitly written into the program. If this happens, then the logic program contains symbols which would not occur in the Horn clauses of ordinary classical logic. An example of this is the cut facility, written !. It will be remembered that the PROLOG interpreter when conducting its searches automatically backtracks in many situations. In some problems, however, we may not wish the program to carry out so much backtracking, which could result in a waste of time, the provision of unnecessary

solutions, and so on. The facility ! controls, in a precise though somewhat complicated way, the amount of backtracking which occurs.
The details of how ! works need not concern us here. An account
of the facility is given in Bratko (1986: ch. 5, pp. 120–36). Bratko
illustrates how ! functions by the following simple, but illuminating
example (1986: 125–6).

Let us begin with a simple PROLOG[9] program for determining
whether X is a member of the list L. This program, which we can
call member.1, is the following:

    member(X, [X | L]).
    member(X, [Y | L]) :- member(X, L).

If, when consulting this program, we make the following query:

    ?- member(X, [a,b,c]).

PROLOG will answer:

    X = a;
    X = b;
    X = c;
    no

Having used its search technique to find one member of the list
[a,b,c], namely a, PROLOG then backtracks to find the next, i.e. b,
and so on until it has found all the members of the list, when it
outputs 'no' to indicate that there are no further solutions. So far
so good, but suppose we are interested in finding only one member of the list—namely, the first member. All the backtracking to
find the remaining members of the list has become redundant, and
can be eliminated using the cut facility ! by changing the program
(member.1) to the following (member.2, say):

    member(X, [X | L]) :- !.
    member(X, [Y | L]) :- member(X, L).

If we repeat the preceding query using the program member.2
instead of the program member.1, we get the following result:

    ?- member(X, [a,b,c]).
    X = a;
    no

In effect the program member.2 finds the first member of the list,
but then does not backtrack to find the other members.

If we compare the logic programs member.1 and member.2, we see that member.1 does indeed consist of a finite set of Horn clauses of 1st-order predicate calculus. The only odd feature is that these are written in a slightly unusual way without using quantifiers, and so on. However, this is a matter of terminology and does not affect anything of substance. By contrast, the logic program member.2 contains the special symbol !, and neither this nor anything like it appears in the Horn clauses of classical 1st-order predicate calculus. This is a simple but vivid and significant illustration of the way in which PROLOG adds to classical logic by introducing elements of control.

Negation-as-failure can be defined in terms of !, and another of PROLOG's control elements: fail, a primitive which simply causes the interpreter to fail. A logic program which defines negation-as-failure is the following:

> not X :- X, !, fail.
> not X.

The program works like this. Given the task of trying to prove not p, it matches to the leftmost part of the first sentence by setting X = p. It then moves on to trying to prove the first part of the right side of the conditional, which with the substitution X = p is simply p. If PROLOG succeeds in proving p, it carries out !, which controls backtracking, and then reaches fail, which causes the whole sentence to fail. Because of the operation of !, the interpreter is not allowed to consider the next sentence—i.e. not X. Thus PROLOG has failed to prove not p. To sum up: if PROLOG can prove p, it fails to prove not p. If, however, PROLOG fails to prove p, then the first sentence fails *before ! is reached*. Backtracking is not therefore prevented, and so the PROLOG interpreter goes on to consider the second sentence not X. By substituting X = p, this sentence enables it to prove not p. Thus, if PROLOG fails to prove p, it succeeds in proving not p. So the logic program does indeed define negation-as-failure. The interesting point here is that negation-as-failure is defined using the control elements ! and fail. Thus PROLOG's non-classical negation arises out of its control elements, and the difference between PROLOG and classical logic regarding negation can be seen as a symptom of the more profound difference that PROLOG introduces control into deductive logic.

Another way in which PROLOG differs from classical (or intuitionistic) logic concerns the order of the premisses. In classical (or intuitionistic) logic, the order in which the premises are written down is of no importance, but this is not the case in PROLOG. Indeed PROLOG will draw quite different conclusions from the same premisses if these are written down in a different order. Again we can illustrate this by a simple example. Consider the following logic program (which we can call 'nonloop'):

p(a).
p(X) :- p(X).

If we make the query ?- p(a)., PROLOG will instantly answer 'yes'. The problem is hardly a very difficult one for PROLOG to solve. It has only to look at the first line of the program, to find out that p(a) is indeed true.

Suppose, however, we had written the two premisses in the opposite order to obtain the following logic program ('loop', say):

p(X) :- p(X).
p(a).

If we made the same query ? - p(a)., there would be a long pause, after which a message such as '∗∗∗ out of memory' would appear. To see what has gone wrong, let us consider how PROLOG would have tackled the same query if the first line of the logic program had been p(X) :- q(X). On examining this line, PROLOG would have reasoned that it could establish its goal of showing that p(a) if it could establish q(a). It would therefore have tried to establish q(a). In the case of the program 'loop', however, p = q, so that the program, having started by trying to prove p(a), ends up by trying to prove p(a), and so gets into a loop. It thus invokes the first line of the program over and over again without ever getting to the second line, which contains the solution of the problem. This simple example shows that the order of the premisses is important because of PROLOG's control system for searching and constructing proofs.

It might be thought from the two preceding examples that in PROLOG one should never write down a clause of the form f :- f. In the logic program 'nonloop', such an expression does no harm but is not needed to answer the query, whereas, in the logic program 'loop', it is a clause of this form which causes the loop. It turns out, however, that there is a very useful facility called 'repeat' which can be defined by the following logic program:

repeat.

repeat :- repeat.

(For technical reasons of speed and efficiency, repeat is usually defined in a way different from the above program, but it behaves exactly as if it was defined in the way just given.) The repeat facility is once again useful in connection with control. As a goal it always succeeds even on backtracking, and each time it is reached by backtracking it generates another alternative execution branch. It is thus useful for handling procedures which have to be carried out many times.

I will conclude this section by returning again to the question of translations of PROLOG into classical logic. This time I will consider the translation methods developed by Gabbay (1993). In his earlier research (1991), Gabbay had shown that many logics (classical or non-classical) can be represented as what he calls *labelled deductive systems*. In such systems any formula such as P(x,y,z) is provided with a label (α, say) to yield a labelled formula α : P(x,y,z). Operations in the logic are then carried out on these labelled formulas. As I have already remarked, the labels can be considered as encoding control instructions, and I will give an example of this in the next chapter. In his 1993 paper, Gabbay suggests methods by which any labelled deductive system can be translated back into classical logic, and in this way presents a thesis of the universality of classical logic. Gabbay's view is that non-classical logics may still be valuable at the human level, but that, for the purposes of computer theorem-proving, his translations of non-classical into classical logic are likely to be useful. My own view is that non-classical logics can, in some circumstances, be appropriate for both humans and computers.

I will now sketch the main idea behind Gabbay's translations, without going into technical details. A predicate such as P(x,y,z) is augmented by the addition of an extra slot to yield a predicate P*(. . .,x,y,z). The label α is placed in this slot, so that, instead of operating with the labelled formula α : P(x,y,z), operations are carried out on P*(α,x,y,z) in a classical two-sorted logic in which α belongs to one sort, and the variables x,y,z to the other.

I will next argue that such a translation method applied to PROLOG is, in the terminology introduced earlier, likely to be formally correct rather than adequate. To begin with, the new predicates will be somewhat bizarre. Suppose we are dealing with a timetable problem. Then P(x,y,z) might say something like there is a train from x to y which leaves x at time z. α, on the other hand, would specify some control instructions about how the predicate is to be handled in the program—e.g. what kind of backtracking is to be used. Thus the new predicate P*(α,x,y,z) would be strange indeed, stating simultaneously some timetable information—e.g. about the times of trains from North Dulwich to London Bridge—and also control instructions about how some PROLOG programs are to be run. This is not very satisfactory. If the original meaning is to be adequately preserved, the timetable information and the control instructions for running programs must surely be kept separate, and handled in different ways. Thus a translation of this type cannot be regarded as adequate, and so does not establish that PROLOG is part of classical logic after all, or even that classical logic is universal. Of course it is true that classical logic has a central importance, but in the next section I will suggest reasons for this which have nothing to do with the possibility of translations into classical logic.

4.6. PROLOG and Certainty: Is Logic *a priori* or Empirical?

I will now consider another difference between PROLOG and classical (or intuitionistic) logic. This concerns not the question of control, but that of certainty. The inferences of classical (or intuitionistic) logic were designed to preserve certainty in the sense that, if the premisses of the inference were certainly true, the conclusion had to be certainly true as well. PROLOG, however, will sometimes draw conclusions which might be false, even though the premisses are certainly true.

This difference is connected with the subject-matter with which the logics were designed to deal. Both Frege (classical logic) and Brouwer (intuitionistic logic) were concerned with the logic appropriate for proofs in the theory of numbers (natural numbers, rational numbers, and real and complex numbers). Frege accepted the standard versions of these theories as correct, whereas Brouwer strove to create new versions which would be even more certain and well founded than the standard ones. Both authors and their followers would have regarded the fundamental axioms of the theories with which they were dealing as certain, and hence it would have seemed reasonable to formulate rules of inference which preserved this certainty. Frege puts the matter quite clearly as follows: 'The aim of proof is . . . to place the truth of a proposition beyond all doubt . . .' (1884: 2).

Let us contrast this with a typical situation in which PROLOG is employed. PROLOG is not used for constructing proofs in formal arithmetic, or real number theory. As we mentioned earlier, it is typically used to construct a system for handling timetable enquiries. Suppose we have to deal with airline flights from a variety of places to a variety of destinations. All the timetable information about when flights depart, when they arrive, and so on can be coded and loaded on to the computer. We now want PROLOG using this database to answer queries such as 'what flights leave London for New York on a weekday afternoon?' It is to answer this kind of query that PROLOG uses negation-as-failure. Suppose it wants to know whether there is a flight leaving London for New York on Wednesday afternoon. It will search through the list of flights leaving London on Wednesday afternoon, and, if none of these flights goes to New York, it will draw the conclusion that there is no flight leaving London for New York on Wednesday afternoon (negation-as-failure). Of course, this conclusion might be false even if the information in the database is, *per impossibile*, certain beyond all reasonable doubt. It could be that, while all the information about flights in the database is correct, information about a flight leaving London for New York on Wednesday afternoon has just been omitted. Yet, although PROLOG's inference here is not certain (it would not satisfy Frege's rigorous criteria), it is highly reasonable, and would be drawn by anyone without a second thought. The key point here is that it would be futile and counter-productive to insist on employing only certainty-preserving rules of inference, if our premises are themselves uncertain. While $5 + 7 = 12$ can be regarded, to all intents and purposes, as certain, no one would regard the information in a timetable as certain. Some flights listed could have been cancelled, or have had their departure times altered, and so on. If the timetable information became too unreliable, it would have, in the limit, to be discarded as useless. In practice this is usually not the case. Timetable information is normally sufficiently reliable to be used as the basis for planning journeys, but no one would regard it as certain. For handling such information, it is obviously appropriate to use a logic which draws reasonable conclusions, even if these are not entirely certain given the data. Thus PROLOG's negation-as-failure is very suitable for timetable (and similar) problems, but would be highly unsuitable for use in making deductions in formal number theory.

What emerges is the idea that there is not a single universal logic, but that different logics may be appropriate in different contexts or problem-situations. It will be interesting, in the light of this, to look again at the question of why the quantum logicians, despite their revolutionary intentions, failed to gain the general acceptance of a new quantum logic; while those working on the logic of artificial intelligence did, more or less inadvertently, change classical (or Fregean) logic. Now classical (or Fregean) logic was essentially the logic of nineteenth-century mathematical analysis, which was, and still is, enormously successful in physics. Quantum mechanics, of course, deals with the micro-world, and has curious features which are not to be found in classical (i.e. nineteenth-century) physics. None the less, from a mathematical point of view, quantum mechanics does not use anything which is not part of the framework of classical mathematics. Schrödinger's equation is a partial differential equation of a standard type, which can be solved using nineteenth-century mathematical methods. Quantum mechanics can indeed be formulated in the more sophisticated framework of Hilbert space (though this is hardly necessary for most practical applications). However, the theory of Hilbert space, though twentieth century, is still, qua mathematical theory, entirely classical, and uses classical (or Fregean) logic. In short, there is nothing in the mathematical apparatus which is actually employed in quantum mechanics to suggest the need for a new logic. Quantum mechanics does indeed have very severe conceptual problems, but these appear to arise so to speak outside the theory's mathematical apparatus, which operates according to traditional and well-understood principles. This, I believe, is the essential reason for the failure of quantum logic. A timetabling problem appears more mundane and less exciting than the problems posed by the strange micro-world of quantum mechanics. Yet it is the mundane timetabling problem which actually requires alterations to classical logic, because the problem is no longer that of drawing certain (or almost certain) conclusions from certain (or almost certain) premises, but that of drawing reasonable (but somewhat unreliable) conclusions from acceptable (but somewhat unreliable) premises.

This analysis also explains why classical logic has a central importance without, however, being universal. Classical logic is the logic which underlies a body of mathematics which has an enormous number of practical applications in physics and other areas. Clearly then classical logic is of very great importance, but it is not universal, because there are application areas for which standard mathematics is not the appropriate tool.

The possibility of a special quantum logic suggested the philosophical thesis that logic is empirical rather than *a priori*. The idea is that we choose not only the mathematics but also the logic which gives the best empirical results in a given domain, and that the logic appropriate to one domain might be different from that appropriate to another. Thus quantum logic might receive empirical support as a means of predicting and explaining results in the microworld, while classical logic was supported empirically in the macroworld. This is how Quine formulates the idea in a famous passage:

Conversely, by the same token, no statement is immune to revision. Revision even of the logical law of the excluded middle has been proposed as a means of simplifying quantum mechanics; and what difference is there in principle between such a shift and the shift whereby Kepler superseded Ptolemy, or Einstein Newton, or Darwin Aristotle? (Quine 1951: 43)

The failure of quantum logic has tended to discredit the view that logic might be empirical, but the successes of PROLOG should lead to its revival and strengthening. In the light of PROLOG, we can say that classical logic is appropriate in domains to which mathematical physics applies, but, in other domains, including many areas of everyday life, a different logical system is appropriate, and produces better results. Thus logic is indeed empirical rather than *a priori*.

5 Can there be an Inductive Logic?

The results of the preceding chapter will now be brought to bear on an old question in the philosophy of science: can there be an inductive logic? Traditionally it was always assumed that logic had two branches—deductive and inductive. However, as we shall see, the development of modern logic from its initiation with Frege in 1879 up to the early 1970s tended to bring about a divergence between deductive and inductive logic. Carnap and Popper, despite their differences, agreed in reducing inductive logic to the theory of confirmation (or corroboration). Now confirmation theory certainly appeared something very different from deductive logic, as that existed in the 1950s and 1960s. So it seemed to many unreasonable to use the term 'logic' to cover both areas. In retrospect this was perhaps the point of maximum divergence between deductive and inductive logic, for the trend towards divergence has been reversed by the new results in artificial intelligence. Machine learning has introduced inductive rules of inference, while PROLOG has introduced control into deductive logic. Now confirmation values can be considered as control elements, and can conveniently be handled using Gabbay's (1991) method of labelled deductive systems. Putting these results together, it has become possible to develop an inductive logic, quite analogous to deductive logic, within the common framework provided by the formula: Logic = Inference + Control. There has thus come about a *rapprochement* between deductive and inductive logic. This has been reinforced by another development—namely, the introduction of confirmation values as part of the control of what is still essentially a deductive logic. This further narrows the gap between deductive and inductive logic, because confirmation values can appear as an ingredient of both. This use of confirmation values appears in Cussens, Hunter, and Srinivasan (1993), and leads to what is perhaps the most original feature of their short, but highly interesting paper. The authors actually carried out an experiment to test out the relative merits of various rival logics. While philosophers have talked in general terms of evaluating logics by their success in different empirical domains, Cussens, Hunter, and Srinivasan (1993) report the first actual experimental investigation of rival logics. Their work thus powerfully supports the empiricist view of logic. I will describe the work of Cussens, Hunter, and Srinivasan in the last two sections of this chapter (5.3 and 5.4). In the next section, however, I will look back in history and examine briefly how the development of deductive logic in the period 1879 to the early 1970s led to an increasing divergence between deductive and inductive logic.

5.1. The Divergence between Deductive and Inductive Logic (up to the Early 1970s)

The development of deductive logic from the time of Frege has seen an increasing emphasis on *rules of inference*. In Frege's original axiomatic deductive approach to logic (1879), the need for rules of inference such as *modus ponens*:

$$A$$
$$A \rightarrow B$$
_____

Therefore   B

was indeed recognized. However, the work of Gentzen in the 1930s eliminated axioms altogether in favour of rules of inference. This approach has seemed more natural to most logicians—hence the term *natural deduction*. The idea is that logic consists essentially of deducing conclusions from premises. This is expressed in a natural way by rules of inference, while the introduction of axioms is an artificial device. A good exposition of logic from this point of view is Tennant's (1978) book, entitled *Natural Logic*. The same approach can be applied to intuitionistic, as well as to standard (classical) logic. To sum up then: there has been an increasing tendency to see deductive logic as consisting of rules of inference. In contrast to this, as I will next argue, rules of inference were, during the same period, almost entirely eliminated from inductive logic.

Let us begin by considering the traditional conception of deductive and inductive logic. Deductive logic was thought to consist of inferences such as

Can there be an Inductive Logic?

> All Men are Mortal.
> Socrates is a Man.
> _____

> Therefore   Socrates is Mortal.

Inductive logic was also thought to consist of inferences, with the difference that these proceeded from a rather indefinite mass of particulars to a general conclusion, e.g.

> Socrates is a Man, and Socrates is Mortal.
> Plato is a Man, and Plato is Mortal.
> Julius Caesar is a Man, and Julius Caesar is Mortal.
>
> . . .
> _____

> Therefore   All Men are Mortal.

This conception was difficult to maintain in the face of Hume's critique of induction, since, as Hume pointed out, the premisses of the inference could all be true, but the conclusion false. An obvious response to Hume was that, although the conclusions of inductive inferences were not certain, they were none the less probable given the premisses. This approach has been developed by the Bayesian school, which actually originated in an attempt to answer Hume (cf. Gillies 1987 for historical details). The development of Bayesianism, however, shifted the problem of inductive logic away from that of inferring inductive conclusions from factual premisses to that of calculating the probability of a hypothesis (h, say) given some relevant evidence (e, say). Research into inductive logic ceased to be an attempt to formulate inductive rules of inference, and became instead an attempt to find ways of calculating $P(h,e)$.

This tendency was reinforced by some further criticisms of induction due to Popper. The following passage, which we quoted in Chapter 1, is particularly notable:

my view of the matter, for what it is worth, is that there is no such thing as a logical method of having new ideas, or a logical reconstruction of this process. My view may be expressed by saying that every discovery contains 'an irrational element', or 'a creative intuition', in Bergson's sense. In a similar way, Einstein speaks of the 'search for those highly universal laws . . . from which a picture of the world can be obtained by pure deduction. There is no logical path', he says, 'leading to these . . . laws. They can only be reached by intuition, based upon something like an intellectual love ('*Einfühlung*') of the objects of experience.' (Popper 1934: 32)

In this passage Popper, following Einstein, denies that there can be any inductive rules of inference having a logical character and which could be used to obtain scientific laws and generalizations. Popper believes that such laws and generalizations can be obtained only by using some irrational creative intuition.

Earlier, in his *Logic of Scientific Discovery* (1934), Popper appears to deny that there can be such a thing as an inductive logic at all. He writes: 'My own view is that the various difficulties of inductive logic here sketched are insurmountable' (Popper 1934: 29).

After the Second World War, particularly in the 1950s, there was a long running intellectual dispute between Carnap and Popper on issues connected with probability and induction. It is usually held that Carnap defended inductive logic and tried to develop it, while Popper attacked inductive logic and claimed that no such thing was possible. However, if we look at the controversy today, it seems (as so often happens when controversies are examined in retrospect) that the opponents had more in common than they perhaps realized at the time. Thus Carnap's *Logical Foundations of Probability* (1950) is often thought of as his classic defence of inductive logic. Yet Carnap writes:

The question whether an inductive logic with exact rules is at all possible is still controversial. But in one point the present opinions of most philosophers and scientists seem to agree, namely, that the inductive procedure is not, so to speak, a mechanical procedure prescribed by fixed rules. If, for instance, a report of observational results is given, and we want to find a hypothesis which is well confirmed and furnishes a good explanation for the events observed, then there is no set of fixed rules which would lead us automatically to the best hypothesis or even a good one. It is a matter of ingenuity and luck for the scientist to hit upon a suitable hypothesis . . . This point, the impossibility of an automatic inductive procedure, has been especially emphasized, among others by Karl Popper . . . who also quotes a statement by Einstein . . . The same point has sometimes been formulated by saying that it is not possible to construct an inductive machine. The latter is presumably meant as a mechanical contrivance which, when fed an observational report, would furnish a suitable hypothesis, just as a computing machine when supplied with two factors furnishes their product. I am completely in agreement that an inductive machine of *this* kind is not possible. (Carnap 1950: 192–3)

It is clear that what Carnap says here is no longer plausible in the light of the recent advances in machine learning, which we described in Chapter 2. However, returning to the 1950s, we can see that Carnap (the defender of inductive logic) and Popper (the opponent of inductive logic) both agreed that it was futile to attempt to formulate inductive rules of inference. Moreover, both Carnap and Popper attempted in the 1950s to develop confirmation theory[1]—that is, a theory which would enable a scientist to calculate (or at least estimate) the degree of confirmation which evidence e gives to a hypothesis h (in symbols C(h,e)). The difference between the two philosophers arises only at this point, for Carnap was a Bayesian and held that C(h,e) obeyed the ordinary axioms of probability, i.e. that it was a probability function, or in symbols that C(h,e) = P(h,e), whereas Popper was a critic of Bayesianism and argued that C(h,e) did not satisfy the axioms of probability (was not a probability function). Although Popper did not think that C(h,e) was a probability function, he none the less held that it could be defined in terms of probability. Thus, for both Carnap and Popper, inductive logic had become confirmation theory, a branch of study which was closely connected with probability theory but had little to do with deductive logic.

To sum up then. By the early 1970s deductive logic was increasingly thought of almost exclusively in terms of rules of inference. By contrast, those working in the field of inductive logic had given up the hope of finding *any* inductive rules of inference, and were trying, using probability theory, to find ways of estimating the degree to which evidence confirmed a hypothesis. This situation represents what is perhaps the maximum divergence between deductive and inductive logic. I will now try to show how the developments in artificial intelligence between 1970 and the present have begun to bring the two fields together again.

5.2. Inductive Logic as Inference + Control

As we saw in Chapter 4, PROLOG introduced control into deductive logic, and thus suggested the formula: Logic = Inference + Control. In terms of this formula, we can explain the divergence between deductive and inductive logic which was discussed in the previous section. In the development of classical (and indeed intuitionistic) logic outside the AI field, attention was largely devoted to the *inference* component. The main problem was that of analysing the logic of mathematical proofs. It was implicitly assumed that these proofs would be constructed by human mathematicians so that not much attention need be paid to issues of control. As we have seen, philosophers of science studying inductive logic concentrated on confirmation theory, which, in terms of our formula, is part of the control component of inductive logic. Suppose we have a number of competing hypotheses. If we can attach confirmation values to the hypotheses, these values will help us to decide which hypothesis to choose for the purpose of making predictions, in practical applications, and so on. Clearly a hypothesis with higher confirmation is, in general, to be preferred to one with lower confirmation. As we observed in our earlier discussion of control (Section 4.4), it is part of the function of the control component to help in the choice, at each stage of the derivation, of the assumptions to be used. Thus confirmation values can be considered as part of the control component of inductive logic. This leads to a neat account of how the divergence between deductive and inductive logic arose, and how it is being overcome by developments in artificial intelligence.

In mathematics, the *control* needed in the construction of a proof was left to the human ingenuity of the mathematician; in science, the *inference* needed was left to the human ingenuity of the scientist. Artificial intelligence has altered this situation by attempting to introduce more automation into both mathematics and science. In mathematics, the study of automated theorem-proving led, as we have seen, to the introduction of *control* into deductive logic; while the attempt to automate inductive inferences in science has led to the introduction of *inference* into inductive logic. This is how a *rapprochement* between deductive and inductive logic has become possible. Both can be brought under the formula: Logic = Inference + Control.

As far as inductive logic is concerned, I have argued that the control component can be identified with confirmation. The development of machine learning has introduced successful inductive rules of inference of a kind which both Carnap and Popper thought to be impossible in the 1950s. The analysis of the machine-learning systems ID3 and GOLEM given in Chapter 2 showed that these systems are based on inductive rules of inference of a broadly logical character, which enable laws and generalizations to be inferred from data and background knowledge. Of course, these were only two examples drawn from the now quite extensive collection of successful machine-learning systems, each one of which can provide examples of inductive rules of inference.

Can there be an Inductive Logic?

In the face of this evidence, it would seem hard to deny that inductive rules of inference do indeed exist. It might, however, still be objected that these rules are not logical in character on the grounds that logical rules of inference should always lead to conclusions which are certain relative to the premisses, whereas the generalizations produced by ID3 and GOLEM remain speculative and conjectural. It is true that the rules of both classical and intuitionistic logic do preserve certainty. However, as we have seen in Chapter 4, PROLOG, when it uses negation-as-failure, gives up the preservation of certainty. Yet the conclusions which PROLOG draws are very reasonable in many applications, and its rules do seem to have a broadly logical character. Given this, it hardly seems sensible to deny that the inductive rules of inference used by ID3 or GOLEM have a logical character.

It remains true, however, that inductive logic is in a much less developed state than deductive logic. There are a whole variety of quite simple and straightforward deductive rules of inference, and these are arranged and classified in well-worked-out schemes. By contrast, successful inductive rules of inference (such as those involved in ID3 or GOLEM) are relatively few in number, and complicated in character. There is as yet, moreover, no scheme for classifying these inductive rules of inference, and showing how they interrelate. This situation should not, however, lead to a denial that there is such a thing as inductive logic, but rather to the conclusion that the area is a promising field for further research.

Research into inductive logic seems to be by nature interdisciplinary. Hitherto this research has concentrated on the development of confirmation theory and has been carried out by two interacting groups—namely, (i) philosophers of science and (ii) students of probability and statistics. The developments we have described suggest that the time has come for an extension of this research programme to include inference as well as confirmation, and a corresponding extension of those involved from two to three interacting groups, i.e. the original two + (iii) students of artificial intelligence (particularly machine learning). As the study of machine learning continues, more successful inductive rules of inference will undoubtedly be discovered. It will, therefore, soon become a matter of urgency to try to classify these rules and show how they interrelate. This is one line of investigation for the extended research programme in inductive logic. It will also be important to investigate how these inductive rules of inference relate to confirmation.

As we have seen, an inductive rule of inference takes the form: 'From K and e, infer h', where K is the background knowledge, e is the evidence, and h is a hypothesis which explains the evidence, in the sense that it is possible to deduce the positive instances from h and K, and, at the same time, not possible to deduce the negative instances from h and K. In general terms, the relation of such a rule to confirmation is straightforward. For the rule to be satisfactory, the confirmation of h given e and K, C(h, e&K), must be high. If there was a generally agreed and fully worked-out theory of confirmation, this would perhaps help us to construct inductive rules of inference, but, of course, things are not so simple. Confirmation theory is still in a somewhat fragmentary and undeveloped state, and, far from there being general agreement as to basic principles, the field is riven by conflicts—most notably the dispute between Bayesians and non-Bayesians. The further study of confirmation theory in connection with machine learning may, however, help to improve this situation rather than making it more confused than ever. Those approaches to confirmation theory which can satisfactorily underpin successful machine-learning programs will gain in plausibility and perhaps be able to suggest further inductive rules of inference for machine learning. Conversely, those varieties of confirmation theory which cannot account for the successes of machine learning will lose plausibility and are likely to be abandoned.

Putting these strands together, we can see that a rich field for research is opening up, and that investigations in this area should result both in improved inductive methods and in an improved understanding of these methods. As yet only a few initial steps in these new lines of research have been taken, and, as the material is rather technical, I will not describe it in detail here.[2]

5.3. Confirmation Values as Control in a Deductive Logic

So far I have emphasized the similarity of deductive and inductive logic in that both can be fitted into the formula: Logic = Inference + Control. However, it might be objected that this leaves a big difference between the two cases, since control in the inductive logic case consists of confirmation values, while in the deductive case, e.g. PROLOG, we have given examples of control, such as the cut !, which appear to be very different from confirmation values. This apparent difference has, however, been eroded by Cussens, Hunter, and Srinivasan (1993), where a *deductive* logic is presented in which confirmation values are used as part of the control.

The work of Cussens, Hunter, and Srinivasan is carried out using Gabbay's (1991) framework of labelled deductive systems. In this approach, labels, for which we shall use roman letters such as i, j, k, l, . . ., are added to formulas such as α, β, γ, . . ., to give labelled formulas, such as i : α. The rules of inference of the logic are augmented with rules for the manipulation of the labels, and the labels can be thought of as encoding control instructions. Gabbay's framework of labelled deductive systems is very useful for formulating non-monotonic logics. Cussens, Hunter, and Srinivasan begin by considering a particular class of non-monotonic logics called *prioritized* logics. They then specialize to what they call *SF* (short for Strong Forward) logics, and then show a way of using confirmation values as the labels in an SF logic to produce what I will call a *confirmation SF* logic. I will now try to explain these various steps in a somewhat imprecise and informal fashion. The full and exact technical details are of course contained in Cussens, Hunter, and Srinivasan (1993).

A prioritized logic allows the inference of the formula with the label that is 'most preferred' according to some preference criterion. In an SF logic, if the labelled formulas are written i : α, j : β, k : γ, . . ., then the labels are partially ordered, and this ordering enables us to establish the required preferences. Roughly speaking, a formula α can be deduced in an SF logic if it is *proposed* but not *defeated*. It is proposed if it can be inferred from the premises using some SF rule of the form i : β → α say. It is defeated if not_α can be deduced from the premises using some other SF rule j : γ → not_α, where j ranks above i in the ordering. Intuitively, then, α can be deduced from the premises, if there is a good argument for α, and no stronger argument for not_α. SF logics are clearly non-monotonic, because, by adding more premises, we can defeat an argument which was previously undefeated.

Let us now see how a confirmation SF logic can be created by using confirmation values to form the labels of an SF logic. In fact Cussens, Hunter, and Srinivasan consider three different ways of estimating confirmation, which they call: *Relative Frequency*, *Bayesian*, and *Pseudo-Bayes*. In what follows, I will describe only the relative-frequency method, partly to simplify the account, but also because, rather surprisingly, the three different methods gave virtually identical results in practice. An SF logic works by assigning labels to formulas of the form $\beta \to \alpha$. We want to use confirmation values to form these labels. Hence we have to suppose that the confirmation of $\beta \to \alpha$ is to be judged relative to some evidence e. Suppose further that e is a sample of N data points. The confirmation is represented, not by a single value, but by a pair of values. The first member of the pair is an estimate of the probability (p, say) of α given β. If β is satisfied at n of the data points in e, and α is satisfied at r of these n points, then the simplest estimate of p is just the relative frequency r/n. This is used as the first of the pair of confirmation values in the relative-frequency method. However, the authors felt it to be necessary to supplement this estimate by a measure of its reliability, and for this they used n/N. For example, if N = 150, then the relative frequency estimate of 1 is more reliable if n = 120 than if n = 2.

We now have the confirmation of $\beta \to \alpha$ represented by an ordered pair of values (i,j), say. To complete the construction of the SF logic we have to impose an ordering on these pairs. Cussens, Hunter, and Srinivasan actually consider two ways in which this could be done (definitions 1 and 2). According to definition 1, (i,j) ranks above (k,l) if and only if i > k, or i = k, and j > l. According to definition 2, (i,j) ranks above (k,l) if and only if i > k, and j >l. Definition 1 imposes a total ordering in which the ordering on the first label takes precedence, and the second label is used only as a 'tie-breaker'. Definition 2 defines a partial order which is a subset of the first relation, and in which both dimensions play an equally important role. The authors do not express a preference for one order rather than the other, but rather consider two confirmation SF logics—namely, Definition 1 using relative frequency, and Definition 2 using relative frequency. Either of these is a completely specified SF logic, and can be used to make non-monotonic deductions from an appropriate database in exactly the same way as, for example, PROLOG with negation-as-failure.

To introduce confirmation values as part of the control of a deductive logic is already something of great interest, but Cussens, Hunter, and Srinivasan carry the investigation further by considering whether it might be possible to decide experimentally, in a particular application, which is the better logic to use—PROLOG with negation-as-failure, or one of their confirmation SF logics. In the next section, I will describe this fascinating attempt to test rival logics experimentally.

5.4. The Empirical Testing of Rival Logics

To carry out their experimental investigation, Cussens, Hunter, and Srinivasan used the machine-learning program GOLEM, which I described in Section 2.4. They applied GOLEM in two areas, the protein domain, which I described in Section 2.6, and the drugs domain, which so far has not been mentioned. To describe their method I will use the protein example with which we are already familiar. However, I will give the results for the drugs domain as well, as they are also interesting. The procedure was exactly the same in the two domains.

It will be remembered that GOLEM is first given some background knowledge K, and a training set of data, and from these generates a set of rules R, say. The rules are then evaluated by a different set of data—the test data. Suppose e is a positive instance from the test data. It has to be checked whether e can be deduced from K and R. However, in order to see whether e can be deduced, some system of logic must be used. GOLEM in fact uses PROLOG with negation-as-failure for this purpose. The idea of Cussens, Hunter, and Srinivasan was to replace PROLOG by a confirmation SF logic during the process of evaluation by the test data, and see whether this resulted in improved performance.

In the protein domain, GOLEM produces rules designed to determine whether a particular position (c, say) in a particular protein is an alpha-helix. This can be written alpha(c). The rules are PROLOG clauses which state a set of conditions which are sufficient for a position X to be an alpha-helix. Thus they take the form alpha(X), if $C_1, \ldots, C_n$, where $C_1, \ldots, C_n$ stand for the set of conditions. An example of such a rule is given in Section 2.6 (GOLEM's Rule 12). If we now let not_alpha (c) mean that position c is not an alpha-helix, then GOLEM can equally well generate rules of the form not_alpha (X), if $D_1, \ldots, D_n$ where $D_1, \ldots, D_n$ stand for a set of conditions sufficient to ensure that X is not an alpha-helix. It is worth noting that the alpha rules and the not_alpha rules are generated by separate runs of GOLEM, and in GOLEM with PROLOG the two predicates are treated as unrelated.

Let GOLEM's background knowledge be K, and the set of rules which it has generated be R, and suppose further that the statement alpha(c) is part of the test data. Suppose we now try to deduce alpha(c) from K and R using PROLOG. The deduction is deemed correct if alpha(c) is deduced, and incorrect if not(alpha(c))[3] is deduced. Because PROLOG uses negation-as-failure, if it fails to deduce alpha(c), then it concludes not(alpha (c)).[3] Thus the two cases: '(i) alpha(c) is deduced, (ii) not(alpha(c)) is deduced' are exhaustive. Similarly if the test data give not_alpha(c) instead of alpha(c), the deduction is deemed correct if not_alpha(c) is deduced, and incorrect if not(not_alpha(c)) is deduced. In this way the deductions can be evaluated as correct or incorrect for each item of the test data, and the overall percentage of correct results calculated. This is termed the *accuracy* of the set of rules.

So far I have described the standard way that GOLEM uses PROLOG to evaluate a set of rules which it has generated. The next step is to repeat the evaluation procedure using a confirmation SF logic instead of PROLOG. To do so, it is necessary to generate both alpha rules, and not_alpha rules, since, as we have seen, SF logics work by comparing the arguments for a proposition (γ, say) with arguments for the negation of γ (not_γ). Some coding of the rules generated by GOLEM is also necessary for the confirmation SF logic to be applicable. Once this is done, the procedure is as follows. If the test data give alpha(c), then the deduction is deemed correct if alpha(c) is deduced, and incorrect if not_alpha(c) is deduced. Similarly if the test data give not_alpha(c), the deduction is deemed correct if not_alpha(c) is deduced, and incorrect if alpha(c) is deduced. However, because negation-as-failure is no longer being used, there is a third possibility in either case—namely, that neither alpha(c) nor not_alpha(c) can be deduced. In this case, we evaluate the situation as neither correct nor incorrect, but *undecided*. The *accuracy* is now defined as the number of correct deductions divided by the sum of the correct and incorrect deductions. Since there may be a number of undecided cases, this sum may be less than the number of members of the set of test data.

There is an analogy here to the difference in the way trials are conducted in England and Scotland. In England if a defendant cannot be proved to be guilty, the verdict is *not guilty*. In other words English law uses negation-as-failure. In Scotland, however, if it is not possible to prove either that a defendant is guilty or that he or she is not guilty, then a third verdict of *not proven* can be given. Clearly, then, the Scots are implicitly using a confirmation SF logic in their legal proceedings!

Some of the experimental details for the protein domain are as follows. The training set consisted of 1,778 examples and the

Can there be an Inductive Logic?

Table 5.1. Comparison of logics in the protein domain (%)

	Correct	Incorrect	Undecided	Accuracy
PROLOG with alpha rules	58	42	0	58
PROLOG with not_alpha rules	59	41	0	59
Definition 1 using relative frequency	53	31	16	63
Definition 2 using relative frequency	45	25	30	64

Table 5.2. Comparison of logics in the drugs domain (%)

	Correct	Incorrect	Undecided	Accuracy
PROLOG with greater rules	79	21	0	79
PROLOG with not_greater rules	80	20	0	80
Definition 1 using relative frequency	70	5	25	93
Definition 2 using relative frequency	70	5	25	93

background knowledge of 6,940 facts. GOLEM generated 100 rules for alpha(X), 99 rules for not_alpha(X), and so 199 rules for use with the confirmation SF logic. The test set contained 322 examples of alpha(X) and 401 of not_alpha(X).

As I remarked above, I will not give precise details of the drugs-domain case. The aim here was to find rules for predicting the relative activity of the drugs, and the basic predicate used was *greater*, meaning having greater activity. The results of the experiment for the protein domain are given in Table 5.1, and for the drugs domain in Table 5.2.

I will now make a few comments on these results. It can be seen that in both domains the use of a confirmation SF logic improved accuracy. The improvement was not great in the protein domain, but quite significant in the drugs domain, where accuracy rose from 79 or 80 per cent to 93 per cent. However, this improvement was obtained at a price. The confirmation SF logic was less decisive than PROLOG, and placed an average of 24 per cent of the cases into the undecided category. One could say that the confirmation

SF logic was more cautious than PROLOG. It would decide a case definitely only if there was fairly strong evidence one way or the other, whereas PROLOG always provided a 'yes or no' answer. The choice of logic thus depends on whether the user is not worried about not getting an answer but wants to make sure that the answer is accurate if one does come up, or whether the user wants to get a definite answer in all cases but is not so worried if the answer is sometimes wrong. The wishes of a particular user are likely to depend on the nature of the application being dealt with. We thus reach a double conclusion. First of all empirical evidence can be brought to bear as to what logic is appropriate in a particular domain. Secondly, a user's choice of logic may depend on the nature of the application and on his or her corresponding wishes and requirements.

All these results are of great theoretical interest and, in particular, give strong and unequivocal support for the empiricist, as opposed to a priori, conception of logic. According to the a priori conception of logic, the truths of logic are known a priori independently of experience. According to the empiricist conception, the truths of logic are established by experience of their successful application. If logic were a priori, we would expect there to be a single universal logic, known independently of experience, and applicable whatever the circumstances. Thus, the very existence of a plurality of logics, one logic being applied in one area, and another in another, already gives support to the view that logic is empirical. However, this argument is not by itself completely decisive. It might be that, although a plurality of logics existed, we could always tell a priori that a particular logic was appropriate for a particular domain by carrying out some kind of a priori analysis of both logic and domain. In the example of Cussens, Hunter, and Srinivasan, however, there seems to be no way in which the relative successes of PROLOG and of the confirmation SF logic in the two domains examined could have been predicted a priori. Only the actual empirical results of the experiment gave an idea of which logic was performing better, and in what way. Moreover, an informed choice of which of these logics to use in a machine-learning system would surely take into account the experimental results obtained. This situation seems to be fatal to the view that logic is a priori.

I concluded Chapter 4 by arguing that the success of PROLOG with its negation-as-failure strongly supported the claim that logic is empirical rather than *a priori*. I can conclude this chapter with the statement that this claim is still further reinforced by the experimental testing of rival logics reported by Cussens, Hunter, and Srinivasan (1993).[4]

6 Do Gödel's Incompleteness Theorems Place a Limit on Artificial Intelligence?

So far in this book we have examined some of the implications which new results in artificial intelligence might have for old questions in the philosophy of science and philosophy of logic. I think it will be agreed that the results have been quite striking. Advances in machine learning have supported the Baconian inductivist view of scientific method against more modern alternatives. The development of PROLOG has provided arguments for the empiricist as opposed to a priori conception of logic, and logic programming has also suggested a new framework for logic within which it may be possible to develop an inductive logic quite similar to deductive logic. Altogether the new results call into question many ideas concerning logic and scientific method which have been dominant for the last fifty or so years.

The interaction between artificial intelligence and the study of logic and scientific method is not, however, all one way. It is both possible and desirable to study what implications, if any, results in logic and scientific method might have for artificial intelligence. I will not, in this chapter, attempt a comprehensive survey of this side of the question, but rather concentrate on a single example—the example which has provoked more discussion than any other. Some of the most famous results in logic (and indeed in mathematics) in the twentieth century are Gödel's incompleteness theorems, the proofs of which were first published in 1931 (see Gödel 1931). Now some thinkers (among others, Lucas, Penrose, and Gödel himself) have argued that these theorems of logic show that there is a limit to what can be achieved by artificial intelligence, and that the human mind can, in some respects at least, go beyond anything which could ever be done by a digital computer.

A Limit on Artificial Intelligence?

One reaction to the claims of Lucas *et al.* might be to ask whether they are really of any great importance. 'After all,' it could be argued, 'even if there is some kind of theoretical limit to what artificial intelligence could ever achieve, it is likely that we are very far from this limit. So research in artificial intelligence can continue quite undisturbed.' This response is, in my view, rather too bland and dismissive. It leaves out of account the important fact that the striking advances in artificial intelligence, just a few of which I have described earlier in the book, are arousing rather mixed feelings. On the one hand, no one is likely to deny that it is a striking human achievement to build computers and to get them to carry out such remarkable feats as discovering new scientific laws. Yet, on the other hand, these very successes raise quite a number of fears and anxieties. Might AI researchers be inadvertently undermining human superiority? Might there come a time when computers are really intellectually superior to human beings, so that human thinking becomes superfluous? If the arguments of Lucas, Penrose, and Gödel are correct, then such fears are quite unfounded. Thus these arguments are certainly worth studying in detail, but, before we do this, it will, I think, be of value to examine more closely some of the anxieties which have been aroused by advances in computing and artificial intelligence. This will be the task of the next section.

6.1. Anxieties Caused by Advances in Artificial Intelligence

The concerns here have been beautifully expressed by Penrose, and I can do no better than quote him:

Over the past few decades, electronic computer technology has made enormous strides. . . . There is something almost frightening about the pace of development. Already computers are able to perform numerous tasks that had previously been the exclusive province of human thinking, with a speed and accuracy which far outstrip anything that a human being can achieve. We have long been accustomed to machinery which easily out-performs us in *physical* ways. *That* causes us no distress. On the contrary, we are only too pleased to have devices which regularly propel us at great speeds across the ground—a good five times as fast as the swiftest human athlete . . . We are even more delighted to have machines that can enable us physically to do things we have never been able to do before: they can lift us into the sky and deposit us at the other side of an ocean in a matter of hours. These achievements do not worry our pride. But to be able to *think*—that has been a very human prerogative. It has, after all, been that ability to think which, when translated to physical terms, has enabled us to transcend our physical limitations and which has seemed to set us above our fellow creatures in achievement. If machines can one day excel us in that one important quality in which we have believed ourselves to be superior, shall we not then have surrendered that unique superiority to our creations? (Penrose 1989: 3–4)

Although not everyone feels in this way about advances in computer technology, Penrose's point of view is widely shared and quite understandable. His point that artificial intelligence may seem to be eroding a hitherto unique human superiority certainly makes sense historically. Consider, for example, Hamlet's famous soliloquy on man (Act II, Scene ii): 'What a piece of work is a man! How noble in reason, how infinite in faculty, in form and moving how express and admirable, in action how like an angel, in apprehension how like a god—the beauty of the world, the paragon of animals! And yet to me what is this quintessence of dust?' In listing the most outstanding human qualities, Hamlet begins: 'how noble in reason!' This agrees very well with the Aristotelian conception of man as the rational animal. Moreover, Hamlet goes on to say: 'in apprehension how like a god! . . . the paragon of animals!' Thus reason and apprehension (understanding) raise human beings above the other animals. But suppose now that computers become able to reason and understand as well as, if not better than, human beings. Will humanity not have lost its leading position? Will human beings not really have become, if not exactly a quintessence of dust, at least a quintessence of neurones, simulable by electronic chips? All this illustrates the profound philosophical implications of artificial intelligence which could well introduce an entirely new, and to some unwelcome, conception of human beings and their relation to the rest of nature.

Penrose is certainly not wrong when he says: 'Already computers are able to perform numerous tasks that had previously been the exclusive province of human thinking . . .' (1989: 3). I earlier quoted the ancient Greek philosopher Democritus as saying that he would 'rather discover one cause than gain the kingdom of Persia' (Diels, Fragment 118, quoted from Freeman 1947: 104). Clearly Democritus thought that intellectual success in scientific discovery was one of the noblest, if not the noblest, human achievement. Yet now computers can discover hitherto unknown laws of nature, as the example of GOLEM given in Chapter 2 shows. Admittedly GOLEM's law is perhaps not so impressive, but then machine learning has only very recently begun to be studied. Who can say what will have been achieved in, for example, fifty years' time?

Another activity in which computers have been very successful is chess-playing. This is obviously not so important as scientific research, but it has considerable significance none the less. For centuries before computers were invented, skill at playing chess was universally admired as a sign of great intelligence. Indeed, in his polemical book *What Computers Can't Do*, published in 1972, just over twenty years ago, Dreyfus expressed considerable doubts as to whether computers would ever be able to play chess skilfully.

Dreyfus argues in his book that, in his own words, 'further significant progress . . . in Artificial Intelligence is extremely unlikely' (1972: 197). The reader may judge of the accuracy of this prognostication by considering the examples given in this book, nearly all of which date from after 1972, while, at the same time remembering that I have been able to give only a few examples from a wide field. Here, however, let us consider the case of chess-playing.

Writing in 1972, Dreyfus is extremely scathing about claims that computers can play chess at all well. This he dismisses as 'scientific mythology'. As he says:

Public gullibility and Simon's enthusiasm was such that Newell, Shaw, and Simon's claims concerning their still bugged program were sufficient to launch the chess machine into the realm of scientific mythology. In 1959, Norbert Wiener, escalating the claim that the program was 'good in the opening', informed the NYU Institute of Philosophy that 'chess-playing machines as of now will counter the moves of a master game with the moves recognized as right in the text books, up to some point in the middle game'. In the same symposium, Michael Scriven moved from the ambiguous claim that 'machines now play chess' to the positive assertion that 'machines are already capable of a good game'.

In fact, in its few recorded games, the Newell, Shaw, Simon program played poor but legal chess, and in its last official bout (October 1960) was beaten in 35 moves by a ten-year-old novice. Fact, however, had ceased to be relevant. (Dreyfus 1972: p. xxxi)

Dreyfus himself was beaten at chess by a computer, and speaks with some sign of irritation of 'the glee with which this victory was announced to the computer community' (1972: Introduction, 223, n. 45). This, however, did not convince him that there was a rosy future for computer chess. He writes:

Embarrassed by my exposé of the disparity between their enthusiasm and their results, AI workers finally produced a reasonably competent program. R. Greenblatt's program called MacHack did in fact beat the author, a rank amateur, and has been entered in several tournaments in which it won a few games. . . . Greenblatt's program has been gradually improved, but it seems to have reached a point of saturation. During the past two years, it lost all games in the tournaments in which it had been entered, and received no further publicity. We shall soon see that given the limitations of digital computers this is just what one would expect. (Dreyfus 1972: pp. xxxii–iii)

But what is the state of the art in computer chess now (1995), twenty-three years after Dreyfus's book?[1] In the human chess world there are about 100 grandmasters, and the best computer chess programs play roughly at the lower edge of the grandmaster level. More specifically, chess players are rated on a scale according to which the World Champion is around 2,800, and there are about 300 players who are evaluated at 2,500 or more. On this scale the best computer program is about 2,550. Thus there are now less than 300 humans who are capable of beating the best computer at chess on a regular basis.

Such is the general position. However, the latest computer chess player, 'Pentium Genius', created a stir by defeating the world champion Garry Kasparov on Wednesday, 31 August 1994.[2] According to an article about this event in the *Guardian* on Friday, 2 September 1994, Kasparov had previously boasted: 'The way things are, I can beat any computer, if I concentrate simply on the computer's style of game. The computer can calculate billions of moves, but it is lacking intuition.' These words have a familiar ring. It will be remembered from the first three chapters of this book that Baconian or mechanical induction was thought to be impossible, because the formulation of new scientific laws required a human creative intuition. Yet laws of nature have now been discovered by computer. Bacon himself would almost certainly have regarded all this praise for the wonders of human intuition as misguided and counterproductive, for he writes: 'The cause and root of nearly all evils in the sciences is this—that while we falsely admire and extol the powers of the human mind we neglect to seek for its true helps' (Bacon 1620: 260).

Returning to computer chess, if the progress of the last twenty or so years continues, then it is not unlikely that, within a few decades, computer chess programs will exist which *no* human is capable of beating. In this area at least, humans would then have surrendered their superiority to their creation; and, if in one area, why not in others? Penrose's anxiety on this question seems to be amply justified.

So far I have discussed the views of those who feel uneasy about advances in computing and artificial intelligence. This is not, however, the whole story. Such is the diversity of human opinions that quite a number of people actually feel pleased at the thought that human intellectual powers might be no better, and perhaps even worse, than those of a large computer. The most famous proponent of this point of view is Alan Turing, who expresses it very clearly in his 1950 article 'Computing Machinery and Intelligence'.

Turing imagines the following situation, which he calls the *imitation game*. An interrogator stands in front of two closed doors. Behind one is a computer and behind the other a human being. The interrogator can communicate with each by means of a teleprinter— that is, he or she can type in a question and will receive after a pause a typewritten answer. The human being has been told to answer in such a way as to help the interrogator. Turing remarks that the best strategy to achieve this would probably be to answer truthfully in all cases. The computer, on the other hand, has been programmed to imitate a human being, and will construct its answers with this end in view, and regardless of truth. Thus, for example, if the interrogator asks the computer to perform a long-division sum, the computer, which could, of course, give the answer immediately, will deliberately delay to simulate a human doing the calculation, and might also introduce a few errors. If asked a question such as 'Do you like strawberries and cream?', the computer might answer 'Yes, very much. I have them for pudding frequently in the summer', even though the computer will obviously never have consumed that dish. The problem for the interrogator is to decide, on the basis of the answers received, which room contains the computer and which the human. If the interrogator is unable in a series of trials to distinguish computer from human at more than chance level, then the computer may be said to have won the imitation game. This has come to be known as the *Turing test* for whether a computer can think in human fashion.

Writing in 1950, Turing made the following prediction: 'I believe that in about fifty years' time it will be possible to program computers, with a storage capacity of about 10^9, to make them play the imitation game so well that an average interrogator will not have more than 70 per cent chance of making the right identification after five minutes of questioning' (1950: 13). Turing's fifty years are almost up, and we can therefore evaluate the success of his prediction. Certainly the storage capacity of about 10^9 can be easily achieved, and, generally speaking, progress in that direction has probably exceeded Turing's expectations. As regards the imitation game, there are now annual competitions for the program which plays the game most successfully, though considerable restrictions on, for example, the subject-matter of the questions are introduced. Thus Turing's prediction, like many AI predictions, contains a great deal of exaggeration, but, none the less, does seem to be on the right lines.

Turing points out that the digital computers which he imagines as playing the imitation game are *discrete state machines*. He explains this concept as follows:

The digital computers considered in the last section may be classified among the 'discrete state machines'. These are the machines which move by sudden jumps or clicks from one quite definite state to another. These states are sufficiently different for the possibility of confusion between them to be ignored. Strictly speaking there are no such machines. Everything really moves continuously. But there are many kinds of machines which can profitably be *thought of* as being discrete state machines. For instance in considering the switches for a lighting system it is a convenient fiction that each switch must be definitely on or definitely off. There must be intermediate positions, but for most purposes we can forget about them. (Turing 1950: 10–11)

Now any discrete state machine can be mimicked exactly by a theoretical computer of the type first described by Turing in his 1936–7 papers and now known as *Turing machines*. A Turing machine is perhaps the simplest type of computer which could be imagined. It has a single tape divided into squares, on each of which a symbol from a finite alphabet can be printed. The machine scans only one square at a time, and can perform only one of a limited number of operations. It can leave the square as it is, or it can erase the symbol and print a new one. It can then move one square to the left, or one square to the right, or stay where it is, or stop. Which operation the machine performs is determined completely by the symbol it views, and the internal state of the machine. Having performed the operation, it is further obliged to move to a new specific internal state. The number of internal states is finite. An important idealization about the machine is that the tape can be indefinitely long. The surprising result which was shown by Turing is that his simple Turing machines can carry out any computation which can be done by any discrete state computer—however complicated its structure, and manner of functioning.

Because of this general result, the mechanist thesis is sometimes formulated as the claim that the human mind is a Turing machine. It is important to note, however, that Turing himself does not use such a formulation. His thesis is that a sufficiently powerful computer could be programmed to play the imitation game successfully—that is, to *simulate* human thinking. The point here is that the human brain may well work continuously, and so not be a discrete state machine. Indeed Turing explicitly considers this possibility as the seventh objection to his thesis. He writes: 'The nervous system is certainly not a discrete state machine. A small error in the information about the size of a nervous impulse impinging on a neuron, may make a large difference to the size of the outgoing impulse. It may be argued that, this being so, one cannot expect to be able to mimic the behavior of the nervous system with a discrete state system' (Turing 1950: 22). Turing does not accept this objection, and replies as follows: 'It is true that a discrete state machine must be different from a continuous machine. But if we adhere to the conditions of the imitation game, the interrogator will not be able to take any advantage of this difference' (1950: 22). In other words, Turing seems to think that, although the brain may not be a Turing machine, its output can none the less be perfectly simulated by a Turing machine. It is on this point that Penrose's views diverge from those of Turing. Penrose agrees with Turing that the brain is not a Turing machine, but thinks that the difference between the two can lead to noticeable effects and can, in particular, allow the brain to outperform any Turing machine in some respects. In contrast to both of them, Gödel thought that the brain was indeed a Turing machine, but that the human brain should not be identified with the human mind, which was, he thought, superior to any Turing machine (including its own brain). It will be seen that there is an interesting spectrum of positions here, and we shall be examining some of them in more detail in the following sections.

It is obvious from the tone of his 1950 article that Turing is not alarmed by the thought of computers equalling or excelling human intellectual performances. On the contrary, he appears to regard this prospect with pleasure and satisfaction. Of course, he is well aware of the very different feelings of many other people, but he describes these sarcastically as what he calls *The "Heads in the Sand" Objection'* (Turing 1950: 15). He formulates this objection as follows:

'The consequences of machines thinking would be too dreadful. Let us hope and believe that they cannot do so.'

This argument is seldom expressed quite so openly as in the form above. But it affects most of us who think about it at all. We like to believe that Man is in some subtle way superior to the rest of creation. It is best if he can be shown to be *necessarily* superior, for then there is no danger of him losing his commanding position. . . . It [the popularity of the argument] is likely to be quite strong in intellectual people, since they value the power of thinking more highly than others, and are more inclined to base their belief in the superiority of Man on this power. (Turing 1950: 15)

Turing does not take the argument at all seriously, and dismisses it with the following ironical words: 'I do not think that this argument is sufficiently substantial to require refutation. Consolation would be more appropriate: perhaps this should be sought in the transmigration of souls' (1950: 15).

Those who hold the opposite view to Turing's have not, however, allowed him to get away with it so easily. On the contrary, Lucas, Penrose, and Gödel, all three of whom studied Turing's ideas closely, have used Gödel's incompleteness theorems to argue that the human mind is in some fundamental ways different from any Turing machine. Obviously to understand their arguments it is necessary to have some grasp of the incompleteness theorems, and so, for those who are unfamiliar with them, I provide a brief informal account in the next section. This can simply be omitted by those already familiar with the theorems, while those who do not yet know them, but would like to see the proofs in full technical detail, can consult Gödel's original (1931) paper, or the more recent accounts in Bell and Machover (1977: 316–60) or Mendelson (1964: 102–58).

6.2. Informal Exposition of Gödel's Incompleteness Theorems

Gödel's incompleteness theorems are concerned with *formal systems* for *arithmetic*. So I will begin by commenting on these terms in the reverse order. Arithmetic is, of course, familiar to everyone from an early age. However, the sense of the word as used in connection with the incompleteness theorems is perhaps a little different from its sense in everyday life. Arithmetic in both senses is concerned with additions like $5 + 7 = 12$, and with multiplications like $6 \times 9 = 54$. However, in the everyday sense, arithmetic includes fractions such as $\frac{3}{4}$, and sometimes also negative numbers. Having a bank balance of $-£3$ might be used as the equivalent of having an overdraft of £3. In what follows, however, arithmetic will be taken to refer only to the so-called *natural numbers*, i.e. 0, 1, 2, 3, . . . So fractions and negative numbers will be excluded. However, the meaning of arithmetic will be extended to include, not just simple additions and multiplications, but also general statements about the natural numbers. An example of such a general statement is the following. Given any natural number n, there is a natural number m such that m is greater than n (m > n), and m is prime. A natural number is said to be prime if the only natural numbers which divide into it exactly are itself and one. From now on we shall use the word 'number' exclusively in the sense of natural number, so that numbers will be restricted to 0, 1, 2, 3, . . . Arithmetic in the sense in which we shall use the term can be considered as the theory of numbers.

Arithmetic in something like this sense appears early in the history of mathematics with the work of the Pythagorean school in ancient Greece. Yet the ancient Greeks, and their successors up to the last two decades of the nineteenth century, treated arithmetic and geometry very differently. Geometry was axiomatized by Euclid in ancient Greek times, and continued to be presented as an axiomatic-deductive system. Yet the Greeks and their successors for many centuries did not even try to present arithmetic as an axiomatic system. The numbers were introduced in an informal fashion, and quite complicated theorems about them were proved, but no one attempted to derive this body of results from a single set of axioms until as late as the 1880s. During the last two decades of the nineteenth century the first axiomatic systems for arithmetic were developed through the efforts of Frege, Dedekind, and Peano (for historical details, see Gillies 1982).

Dedekind presented his axiomatic system informally, just as Euclid had done. Frege and Peano, however, endeavoured to create fully formalized axiom systems for arithmetic. In such a *formal system*, the axioms are stated in a symbolic language more precise than ordinary language, and each step in the proof of a theorem has to be justified by appeal to a small number of precisely stated rules of inference.

The work of Frege and Peano was continued by Russell and Whitehead, who produced in three enormous volumes, published between 1910 and 1913, a famous formal system called *Principia Mathematica*, or *PM* for short.[3] This system was of great interest for the following reason. Its axioms were claimed to be truths of logic, and it was also thought by its authors that it should be possible to prove any theorem of mathematics within *PM*. Had this in fact been true, then it would have been shown that the whole of mathematics is nothing but an extension of logic. This claim is known as the *logicist* philosophy of mathematics. Of course, Russell and Whitehead could not literally prove within *PM* all the theorems even of existing mathematics, let alone of all future mathematics. In their three massive volumes, however, they did prove a very large number of mathematical theorems, so that by the end of volume iii it did begin to look plausible that it would be possible to prove any further mathematical theorem within their formal system. Gödel, however, managed to construct a true statement of arithmetic which could not be proved within *PM* (assuming that *PM* satisfied some conditions which will be stated later). He thus showed that the logicist philosophy of mathematics of Russell and Whitehead was not correct.

The relation of Gödel's incompleteness theorems to the logicist philosophy of mathematics of Russell and Whitehead is clearly indicated by the title of Gödel's (1931) paper, which runs 'On Formally Undecidable Propositions of Principia Mathematica and Related Systems I'. However, as the title also shows, his results do not apply just to *PM*, but to any similar formal system. I am now in a position to state the first of Gödel's incompleteness theorems, or rather a later version of the theorem proved by Rosser (1936), and sometimes known as the Gödel–Rosser theorem.[4] The theorem will be stated not for *PM*, but for an arbitrary formal system S, satisfying some specified conditions.

> *Gödel's First Incompleteness Theorem.* Given any formal system S, such that (1) S is consistent and (2) a sufficiently large amount of arithmetic can be derived in S, then we can find an undecidable proposition p in S—that is to say, a proposition p such that p cannot be proved in S, and the negation of p (not-p)

123

also cannot be proved in S. p can, however, be shown to be a true statement of arithmetic by an informal argument outside S.

A few comments on this are in order. The first condition that S should be consistent means that we cannot derive a contradiction of the form p & not-p in S. Since we are assuming that the underlying logic of S is ordinary classical logic, if S is inconsistent, then it can be shown that any proposition whatever can be proved in S, for, in classical logic, anything follows from a contradiction. This means that inconsistent systems with classical logic are effectively useless. The second condition states that a sufficiently large amount of arithmetic can be derived in S. The meaning of 'sufficiently large' here can be specified precisely in a full technical version of the theorem.

Now how do we set about proving such a remarkable theorem? Gödel himself says that the idea of the proof is closely related to the liar paradox (Gödel 1931: 149). So let us follow up this clue. One form of the liar paradox arises by considering the following sentence:

This sentence is false.

A little reflection will convince the reader that, if the above sentence is true, then it is false, and, if it is false, then it is true. This is a contradiction. So, if we are to have a consistent language, we must formulate rules which forbid the formation of such paradoxical sentences.

Now Gödel's idea was to construct a sentence similar to that in the version of the liar paradox just given, but which resulted, not in a contradiction, but in establishing an undecidable formula for S. The sentence in question is roughly speaking the following:

This formula is not provable in S.

Call this sentence p. If p is provable in S, then we can derive a contradiction, since p says that it is not provable in S. But by assumption S is consistent, and so p is not provable in S. This argument is rough and informal, but it can be formalized in the full technical proof of Gödel's theorem. Incidentally, we can now conclude that p must be true, since p says that it is not provable in S, and that is indeed the case.

To complete the proof of the first incompleteness theorem, we have also to show that the negation of p (not-p) is also not provable in S. This turns out to be a little harder, and so I will not explain the proof informally. In order to show that not-p was not provable in S, Gödel had to assume that S was not just consistent, but what he called ω-consistent. ω-consistency is a stronger condition than consistency, in the sense that, if a system is ω-consistent, it is consistent, but not necessarily vice versa. By changing the form of the undecidable sentence from p to something a little more complicated, Rosser (1936) was able to show that the original theorem could be proved assuming only consistency. The difference between Gödel's original theorem and the Gödel–Rosser theorem is very clearly explained by Mendelson (1964: 142–7). Mendelson also explains the difference in the intuitive interpretations of Gödel's original undecidable sentence, and the undecidable sentence used by Rosser.

At this point, I must confess that, in the interests of simplifying this informal account, I propose to do a little cheating. I will consider the undecidable sentence in the original Gödel form given above—i.e. this formula is not provable in S—rather than in Rosser's more complicated undecidable sentence. At the same time I will take the first incompleteness theorem in the stronger Gödel–Rosser form in order to avoid the problem of considering the more complicated condition of ω-consistency rather than the simpler condition of consistency. The reader will quickly perceive that this procedure is not strictly correct, but it should not lead to any serious misconceptions.

So far we have shown that, if we can produce a statement which asserts that it is not provable in S, we can establish the theorem. But how can we possibly produce such a statement? S, it will be remembered, is a formal system for deriving statements of arithmetic —i.e. statements about numbers. How can such a statement say that it is not provable in S? To achieve such a thing, we have to make use of a second highly ingenious idea of Gödel's. Gödel introduced a kind of code which associates a number with every statement of S. There is a rule which enables us to derive the statement from the number and another which enables us to obtain the number from the statement. This process of assigning numbers to statements is now known as *Gödel numbering*. Let us see roughly how it works in a simple example taken from ordinary language rather than a formal system.

Consider then the following:

the cat sat on the mat

A Limit on Artificial Intelligence?

Let us associate numbers with letters according to the following scheme:

```
a c e h m n o s t
1 2 3 4  5 6 7 8 9
```

Let us further use the number 0 to stand for the blank between words. We can then associate our familiar sentence about the cat with the following number:

9430219081907609430519

Conversely, if we wanted to obtain the original sentence from the above number, we would first look for the 0's, and this would break the number up into numbers corresponding to words. We would then use the correlation of numbers with letters of the alphabet to recover the words.

The process can easily be extended from a single sentence to two or more sentences. Suppose, for example, we have the following two sentences:

the cat sat on the mat. the cat chats.

(To avoid complications, I am adopting the e. e. cummings convention of omitting capital letters.) To code these two sentences into a single number, we need only stipulate that two zeros in succession (00) stand for the full stop. The number of the two sentences is then easily seen to be

9430219081907609430519009430219024198 00

Recovering the original sentences from the number is again easy. We first look through the number, and pick out the double zeros (00). This breaks the number down into numbers corresponding to sentences. We then in each sentence-number look for the zeros, and this breaks it into word-numbers. Finally we use the correlation between numbers and letters to recover the original words.

It might be objected that the method I have sketched applies only to sentences composed out of the nine letters given earlier. This is true, but the method can easily be extended to the full alphabet, and also to capital letters, if these are thought to be desirable. We normally write numbers to the base 10, and correspondingly use ten numerals 0, 1, 2, . . ., 9. However, numbers can be expressed to any base we like. In the alphabet there are twenty-six letters. If we have capitals as well, this gives fifty-two. We might like to add punctuation marks such as single and double inverted commas (two symbols in each case), comma, colon, semi-colon, and question mark. This makes sixty basic symbols. So, if we express our numbers to the base 61, we will have a numeral for each basic symbol, and can use the above method to write down a number corresponding to any sequence of English sentences. For example, we can write down a number corresponding to George Eliot's *Middlemarch*. Lest someone mystically minded might wish to associate the mathematical properties of this number with the literary qualities of the novel, it should be pointed out that the coding (or Gödel numbering) can be done in a whole variety of different ways, and I have here given only one simple example.

Returning to our formal system S, once we have carried out a Gödel numbering of all the expressions, formulas, and sequences of formulas, we are in a position to translate statements about the formal system S into statements of arithmetic. Let us see roughly how this can be done, using a simple example. Consider then the statement that A is a theorem of S. A will have a Gödel number, call it m. Then the statement becomes: there is a number n such that n is the Gödel number of a proof in S of the formula with Gödel number m. To check whether a particular number n is the Gödel number of a proof in S of m, we must first check whether n breaks up into a sequence of numbers corresponding to formulas. The last of these numbers has to be m. Every earlier number in the sequence must either be the number of an axiom, or the number of a formula which follows from earlier formulas in the sequence using one of the rules of inference. Since the rules of inference are themselves numbered, checking whether this last possibility holds again reduces to checking whether particular numbers are related in a particular fashion. In this way the statement that A is a theorem of S becomes translated into a statement about numbers, which can be checked by arithmetical techniques. But now we are assuming that a sufficiently large amount of arithmetic can be derived in S. If this is the case, then we will be able to express the arithmetical statement corresponding to 'A is a theorem of S' as a formula of S itself. The general procedure here is the following. We start with a statement about S. We then use the Gödel numbering to translate this into a statement of arithmetic, and we then express this statement of arithmetic by a formula in S. The reader will now see that all we have to do is apply this general procedure to the statement p—i.e. this formula is not provable in

S—and we will have obtained an undecidable formula of S. I will now show in more detail how this can be done.

At this point we have to make use of a traditional concept of logic, already discussed in Chapter 2. This is the notion of a 1-place predicate. This idea is already to be found in Aristotelian logic, and so we can illustrate it with the familiar example: 'Socrates is mortal'. This is analysed into a subject: Socrates, and a predicate: '. . . is mortal'. It is convenient to write predicates using variables such as x, y, z, . . ., so that this example becomes: 'x is mortal'. Of course, we can have such predicates for numbers as well as for human beings—e.g. x is even, x is prime, and so on. We can also, though this was not done in the ancient world, introduce predicates with two variables. Thus corresponding to: 'Socrates is older than Plato', we have: 'x is older than y'; corresponding to: '5 is greater than 3', we have: 'x is greater than y', and so on. If a predicate has only one variable, it is known as a 1-place predicate; if it has two, a 2-place predicate. In a similar fashion we can introduce predicates with 3, 4, or indeed any number of places. For Gödel's theorem, however, it will be sufficient to consider just 1-place predicates.

A 1-place predicate, such as 'x is mortal', could be written 'x is P', but it is more convenient to use the notation: '$P(x)$'. Now S, our formal system, will have a lot of 1-place predicates of numbers. Our earlier examples—'x is even', 'x is prime'—will certainly be there, along with many others. Now these 1-place predicates will have Gödel numbers. If n is the Gödel number of such a predicate, we can denote it by $P_n(x)$. Using this notation, we can next introduce another 1-place predicate of numbers, namely $P_x(x)$. This is true of a number n if n is the Gödel number of a 1-place predicate $P_n(x)$, and $P_n(n)$ is true; otherwise the predicate is false of the number. In terms of $P_x(x)$, we can define yet another 1-place predicate ($R(x)$, say) as follows:

$R(x)$ = For all numbers n, n is not the Gödel number of a proof in S of $P_x(x)$

Now $R(x)$ is a 1-place predicate of numbers. So, if a sufficiently large amount of arithmetic can be derived in S, then S will contain $R(x)$ as one of its predicates of numbers. These predicates each have a Gödel number. So, let the Gödel number of $R(x)$ be k. Then $R(x) = P_k(x)$. So we have:

$P_k(x)$ = For all numbers n, n is not the Gödel number of a proof in S of $P_x(x)$

x is here a variable which ranges over numbers. So we can substitute k for x, to obtain:

$P_k(k)$ = For all numbers n, n is not the Gödel number of a proof in S of $P_k(k)$

But now we are done. $P_k(k)$ is an arithmetical sentence of S, but, by the right-hand side of the above equation, it can be interpreted as saying that it is unprovable in S. Thus, by the argument sketched earlier, $P_k(k)$ is an undecidable proposition, and Gödel's first incompleteness theorem is proved.

Before going on to consider Gödel's second incompleteness theorem, I would like to make two further comments on the proof I have just sketched. First of all some readers may still be worried about the consideration of a formula of S which says that it is unprovable in S. Gödel himself compared this to the liar paradox, and there is indeed a similarity; but does not this mean that the Gödel sentence is itself illegitimate and paradoxical, just like the sentence of the liar paradox? The answer to this objection is that the undecidable sentence $P_k(k)$ is just a complicated sentence about numbers. It is only when we introduce a particular coding using Gödel numbers that $P_k(k)$ can be interpreted as saying that it is unprovable in S. With a different coding, $P_k(k)$ would no longer say that it was unprovable in S, though, of course, there would be another undecidable sentence relative to this new coding. These considerations show that there is nothing about the sentence $P_k(k)$ itself which could give rise to paradoxes.

My second comment is a qualitative point about the general character of the proof. Starting with a formal system S in which a sufficiently large amount of arithmetic can be derived, the aim of the proof is to produce a proposition about numbers which is true and yet undecidable within S. Metaphorically speaking we achieve this goal by, as it were, standing outside S and considering S as a whole. This enables us to see that something is true which cannot be decided *from within* S. This feature of 'looking at S as a whole from the outside' appears in the definition of the undecidable sentence. This says that, for all numbers n, n is not the Gödel number of a proof in S of $P_k(k)$, and so makes implicit reference to all proofs in S. This reference to all proofs in S carries, in turn, the implication of looking at S from the outside. I mention this aspect of the proof because it will be important when we consider how Gödel's incompleteness theorems might be applied to the problem of minds and machines.

A Limit on Artificial Intelligence?

I will now conclude the present section with a brief sketch of Gödel's second incompleteness theorem. It will be remembered that Gödel's first incompleteness theorem refuted the *logicist* philosophy of mathematics of Russell and Whitehead. His second incompleteness theorem refuted another major philosophy of mathematics of the time. This was the *formalist* view held by the German mathematician David Hilbert and his followers at Göttingen. Russell and Whitehead thought that any theorem of mathematics could be formulated and proved within one grand formal system whose axioms were just axioms of logic. In this way they hoped to reduce mathematics to logic. Hilbert also thought that mathematics should be formalized, but he was prepared to allow a variety of formal systems rather than just one. Indeed, there would be different formal systems for each of the branches of mathematics, such as arithmetic, geometry, set theory, and so on. Moreover, the axioms of these formal systems would not be axioms of logic, but axioms appropriate to the subject-matter in hand—e.g. axioms of arithmetic. In order to prevent any contradictions arising in mathematics, Hilbert thought it was most important to prove that these various formal systems were consistent. Moreover, he stipulated that such consistency proofs should use only the methods of very elementary arithmetic. Since very elementary arithmetic appears to be plainly consistent, this procedure would provide a firm foundation for mathematics. The attempt to produce such consistency proofs was known as *Hilbert's programme*, and he and his followers were working on it in the early 1930s when Gödel's second incompleteness theorem showed that the programme could not, after all, be carried out. If we let S, as previously, be a formal system in which a sufficiently large amount of arithmetic can be derived, then the theorem can be stated as follows.

> *Gödel's Second Incompleteness Theorem.* If S is consistent, then the consistency of S cannot be proved within S itself.

It is easy to see why this shows the impossibility of carrying out Hilbert's programme. Let S be some complicated formal system for some branch of mathematics—e.g. set theory. Certainly we will be able to formulate very elementary arithmetic within S, and so we will not be able to prove S consistent using only the methods of elementary arithmetic, as Hilbert had hoped.

I will now sketch the proof of Gödel's second incompleteness theorem. Consider the statement that S is consistent. This is equivalent to saying that there do not exist numbers m and n, such that n is the Gödel number of a proof of some formula A of S, while m is the Gödel number of a proof of the negation of A (not-A). Now, using the methods employed in the proof of the first incompleteness theorem, we can translate this into a statement of arithmetic, which can then be expressed as a sentence of S. Let this sentence be Cons(S). Further let p be the undecidable sentence of S which occurs in the proof of the first incompleteness theorem (i.e. $P_k(k)$). It follows from the first incompleteness theorem that, if S is consistent, then p is not provable in S. But

p = p is not provable in S

We can thus translate: 'If S is consistent, then p is not provable in S' into the following statement of S: 'If Cons(S), then p'. Moreover, by going through the full formal proof of the first incompleteness theorem, and translating it into S, which we can do since the proof involves only arithmetical notions, we obtain a proof in S of the statement: 'If Cons(S), then p'. Now suppose that we can prove the consistency of S within S. We can then obtain a proof of Cons(S) within S, but we already have a proof of 'If Cons(S), then p' within S. So we obtain a proof of p within S. However, by the first incompleteness theorem, if S is consistent, then p cannot be proved within S. So, if S is consistent, then the consistency of S cannot be proved within S.

We have seen that Gödel's incompleteness theorems refuted two major philosophies of mathematics. Do they also refute the mechanist thesis that the human mind is no better than a powerful computer? This is the question to which we must now turn.

6.3. The Lucas Argument

In a now famous article (Lucas 1961), Lucas attempted to use Gödel's first incompleteness theorem (which he refers to simply as Gödel's theorem) to show that mechanism is false. His aims are clearly stated in the opening paragraph which runs as follows:

Gödel's theorem seems to me to prove that Mechanism is false, that is, that minds cannot be explained as machines. So also has it seemed to many other people: almost every mathematical logician I have put the matter to has confessed to similar thoughts, but has felt reluctant to commit himself definitely until he could see the whole argument set out, with all objections fully stated and properly met. This I attempt to do. (Lucas 1961: 43)

Lucas gives various formulations of the argument. Here is one:

However complicated a machine we construct, it will, if it is a machine, correspond to a formal system, which in turn will be liable to the Gödel procedure for finding a formula unprovable-in-that-system. This formula the machine will be unable to produce as being true, although a mind can see that it is true. And so the machine will still not be an adequate model of the mind. We are trying to produce a model of the mind which is mechanical—which is essentially 'dead'—but the mind, being in fact 'alive', can always go one better than any formal, ossified, dead system can. Thanks to Gödel's theorem, the mind always has the last word. (Lucas 1961: 48)

This argument, or something sufficiently similar to it, I will call the *Lucas argument*.[5] It has given rise to an immense amount of discussion, and in this section, and the next two, I will try to expound some of the main strands in the debate. Let me begin with a preliminary point. It is worth noting that Lucas assumes that any machine (by which he means a discrete state machine) can be represented by a formal system. As he says: 'it will, if it is a machine, correspond to a formal system . . .' (Lucas 1961: 48). I propose to call this the *representability assumption*, and will raise some questions about it in Section 6.5. For this section and the next, however, I will regard it as unproblematic, which seems indeed to be the opinion of most writers on this topic.

Lucas has sometimes emphasized that his argument is best stated in dialogue form. This form of the argument is perhaps indeed the clearest, and has the additional advantage that it enables us to relate the argument to Turing's imitation game. Here then is one version of the dialogue form of the argument:

For the mechanist thesis to hold water, it must be possible, in principle, to produce a model, a single model, which can do anything the mind can do. It is like a game. The mechanist has first turn. He produces a—*any*, but only a *definite one*—mechanical model of the mind. I point to something which it cannot do, but the mind can. The mechanist is free to modify his example, but each time he does so, I am entitled to look for defects in the revised model. If the mechanist can devise a model that I cannot find fault with, his thesis is established: if he cannot, then it is not proven: and since—as it turns out—he necessarily cannot, it is refuted. (Lucas 1961: 50)

It is clear that the conditions of Lucas's game are very different from those of Turing's imitation game. Lucas requires that he be given by the mechanist a full specification of the machine which is supposed to be equivalent to his (Lucas's) mind. Lucas then refutes the mechanist by carrying out the Gödel argument for this specification, and so producing as true the undecidable sentence p which the machine is unable to prove. Under the conditions of the imitation game, however, the interrogator is not presented with a specification of the machine—indeed the machine is hidden behind one of the two closed doors. Thus the Lucas argument is not directly relevant to the imitation game, and this may be one reason why Turing did not take this type of argument very seriously.

We can clarify this point by imagining that Lucas is acting as the interrogator in the imitation game. Behind one closed door is a machine designed by the mechanist to play the game, while behind the other door there might be, for example, my colleague, the mathematical logician Moshé Machover. Let us suppose that, after the allowed five minutes of questioning, Lucas makes a mistake and judges that the computer is the human. At this point Lucas might say: 'You have certainly succeeded in fooling me with your imitation game, but it is still an easy matter to demonstrate using my argument that your machine is not the same as the human mind of Moshé Machover. To do so, you must present him with a full specification of your machine, its programs, etc. Moshé Machover can then settle down with this material, work through the Gödel argument, and so produce as true a proposition p (the Gödelian undecidable proposition), which your machine will not be able to prove. This will show that your machine is not identical with the mind of Moshé Machover, even though I was deceived by the conditions of the imitation game into confusing the two.' This little thought experiment has, I hope, shown the considerable difference between the imitation game and the Lucas argument.

Perhaps the earliest objection to the Lucas argument came from Putnam (1961: 77). Putnam had formulated the argument independently of Lucas, but had discussed it with Lucas when they met in Princeton in 1957. Putnam's attitude to the argument was, however, the opposite of Lucas's. Far from wanting to defend the argument, his aim was to show that it is wrong. Putnam formulated both the argument and his objection to it in terms of Turing machines. Restating his point in terms of formal systems, it comes out like this. Suppose we have a machine which is represented by a formal system S. Then a human observer (Lucas say) can show from Gödel's first incompleteness theorem that, if S is consistent, then p is true, where p is the undecidable proposition associated with S. However, as Putnam observes, the same can be proved within S. Indeed, as we saw in the previous section, it is possible to prove within S the equivalent statement: if Cons(S), then p. Lucas can prove that p is true—thus getting the better of the machine— only if he can prove that S is consistent, but he is no more capable of doing this than the machine.

This objection has been often repeated subsequently, but it does seem that some answers to it can be given. Although it might indeed be difficult to give a full consistency proof for the relevant formal system S, it might none the less be possible to give some quite convincing reasons for supposing that S is consistent. For example, our intuitions about the natural numbers do strongly suggest that a considerable variety of axiomatic systems for arithmetic are consistent. There are other formal systems—e.g. versions of axiomatic set theory such as ZFC—which many mathematicians have been working in for many decades. If such a system were inconsistent, it seems likely that a contradiction would have come to light by this time, and this gives a good reason for supposing that the formal system is indeed consistent. It is worth noting, moreover, that Lucas does not say that we can prove that the Gödel sentence p is true, but only that we can 'produce it as true'. By this he seems to mean that the human mind can produce informal, intuitive, but still convincing, reasons for supposing that p is true (like those just given), while the machine, which has to rely on formal proof, can do no such thing. Lucas also gives another formulation of his argument designed to overcome the objection about our ignorance of the consistency of S. I will state this in the next section.

Sections 6.4 and 6.5 will be devoted to considering objections to the Lucas argument, but, before coming to these, it will be interesting to consider what consequences follow if we accept the argument as being correct. The first such consequence would seem to be that the human mind is, in some fundamental respects, superior to any possible computer. After all the human mind, according to the argument, is always capable of going beyond what any given computer can do and of producing as true a statement which for the computer is undecidable. This surely shows a superiority to the computer. Lucas, however, states explicitly that he is not arguing for the superiority of mind to machine. As he says:

We are not discussing whether machines or minds are superior, but whether they are the same. In some respects machines are undoubtedly superior to human minds; and the question on which they are stumped is admittedly a rather niggling, even trivial, question. But it is enough, enough to show that the machine is *not the same* as a mind. True, the machine can do many things that a human mind cannot do: but if there is of necessity something that the machine cannot do, though the mind can, then, however trivial the matter is, we cannot equate the two, and cannot hope ever to have a mechanical model that will adequately represent the mind. (Lucas 1961: 49)

Despite this explicit denial, the tone of other passages by Lucas suggests that he does, after all, regard the human mind as superior to the computer. We have already quoted him as saying: 'the mind, being in fact "alive", can always go one better than any formal, ossified, dead system can' (Lucas 1961: 48), and in a later paper he writes: 'The mechanist, regarding men as something less than men, namely machines, . . .' (Lucas 1968a: 148). Surely these last two passages imply a superiority on the part of the human mind, which does indeed seem to me a natural consequence of accepting the Lucas argument.

The Lucas argument also seems to lend support to dualism. After all, if the human mind can always go one better than a material artefact like a computer, then it seems natural to suppose that the mind has a different character, or substance, from matter. Once again, however, Lucas does not draw a seemingly natural conclusion from his argument, but writes: 'This is not enough to re-establish traditional dualism—which seems to me open to many philosophical objections . . .' (Lucas 1968b: 156).

This is a convenient moment to compare Lucas's views with those of Gödel, for Gödel, as we shall see, advocated both dualism and the thesis that human minds are superior to computers. Gödel did indeed conclude that his incompleteness theorems showed that mechanism is false, though his argument for this conclusion was, as we shall see, somewhat different from Lucas's. Gödel may have reached these conclusions quite soon after proving his theorems, but, unless the manuscripts he left behind shed further light on the question, this must remain a speculation, since his views appeared in print only in 1974, thanks to the efforts of Hao Wang. Wang had a series of meetings with Gödel, starting in October 1971, in which they discussed a number of issues, including the question of minds and machines. Wang then published in 1974, with Gödel's approval, an account of these discussions, which included some formulations drawn up by Gödel (see Wang 1974: 324–6). Wang discusses the issue again in a later article (Wang 1993), which includes some further material from his discussions with Gödel. On the basis of Wang's account, it is possible to reconstruct Gödel's own views on the question of minds and machines.

Wang gives the following formulation by Gödel himself, of what seems to have been Gödel's central argument for the conclusion that minds are not machines. It runs as follows: 'Either the human mind surpasses all machines (to be more precise: it can decide more number theoretical questions than any machine) or else there exist number theoretical questions undecidable for the human mind' (Wang 1974: 324). Wang comments:

Gödel thinks Hilbert was right in rejecting the second alternative. If it were true it would mean that human reason is utterly irrational by asking questions it cannot answer, while asserting emphatically that only reason can answer them. Human reason would then be very imperfect and, in some sense, even inconsistent, in glaring contradiction to the fact that those parts of mathematics which have been systematically and completely developed (such as, e.g. the theory of 1st and 2nd degree Diophantine equations, the latter with two unknowns) show an amazing degree of beauty and perfection. In these fields, by entirely unexpected laws and procedures (such as the quadratic law of reciprocity, the Euclidean algorithm, the development into continued fractions, etc.), means are provided not only for solving all relevant problems, but also solving them in a most beautiful and perfectly feasible manner (e.g. due to the existence of simple expressions yielding *all* solutions). These facts seem to justify what may be called 'rationalistic optimism'. (Wang 1974: 324–5)

Gödel's argument seems to me definitely distinct from Lucas's. On the one hand, it is more logically rigorous, and not liable, for example, to Putnam's objection, or to the objections I will deal with in the next two sections. If the human mind can indeed decide all number theoretical questions, then it must surpass any machine, for, given any particular machine, there will certainly be number theoretical questions which that machine cannot decide. Note too that this yields an unequivocal statement of the superiority of the human mind to any computer. On the other hand, however, Gödel's argument depends on a much stronger premiss than any which Lucas uses. Gödel assumes that the human mind can decide all number theoretical questions, and this is surely distinctly dubious.

On this point, Gödel is following Hilbert, who, in 1900, advocated the 'rationalistic optimism' that any clearly formulated mathematical problem would one day be solved. This was in connection with the list of problems which Hilbert proposed as suitable for the mathematical community to work on. There is a certain irony in the fact that Gödel, who refuted Hilbert's formalist philosophy of mathematics, should support him in this optimistic view. Certainly not all leading mathematicians did so. Indeed Brouwer wrote, referring to Hilbert: 'There is not a shred of a proof for the conviction, which has sometimes been put forward that there exist no unsolvable mathematical problems' (Brouwer 1908: 109). The fate of the very first in Hilbert's 1900 list of problems seems to support Brouwer's view rather than Gödel's.

Hilbert's first problem was to decide on the truth of Cantor's continuum hypothesis. However, subsequent research, including some of Gödel's, seems to indicate that this problem is not soluble. More precisely, Gödel showed that the truth of the continuum hypothesis is consistent with the remaining axioms of set theory (see Gödel 1940). Cohen demonstrated in 1963–4 that the falsity of the continuum hypothesis is consistent with the remaining axioms of set theory (see Cohen 1966). So the truth of the continuum hypothesis is not decidable on the basis of the currently accepted axioms of set theory. Of course, this does not show that the continuum hypothesis is undecidable in some absolute sense. Indeed, Gödel suggests in his 1963 article that it may be possible to devise new axioms which would settle the question. As he says: 'one has good reason for suspecting that the role of the continuum problem in set theory will be to lead to the discovery of new axioms which will make it possible to disprove Cantor's conjecture' (Gödel 1963: 480). More than thirty years have now passed since 1963, but no new axioms of this kind have appeared. Moreover, even if new axioms were suggested which decided the continuum hypothesis one way or the other, it seems to me more likely that these new axioms would themselves become the centre of a dispute than that they would be regarded as having definitively solved the continuum problem.

It might be objected that, for his argument about minds and machines, Gödel requires only that all questions of number theory be decidable by the human mind, not that all mathematical questions (including questions of set theory) be so decidable. Yet even number theory contains many highly complicated problems whose ultimate solution is very far from being a foregone conclusion.

Moreover, the problems of set theory cannot be put entirely aside, since, as Gödel himself remarks, results in set theory have consequences in number theory. Indeed, speaking of strong axioms of infinity, Gödel says: 'It can be proved that these axioms also have consequences far outside the domain of very great transfinite numbers, which is their immediate subject matter: each of them, under the assumption of its consistency, can be shown to increase the number of decidable propositions even in the field of Diophantine equations' (Gödel 1963: 477).

Returning then to Gödel's argument for the superiority of minds to machines, my conclusion is that it is based on a premiss—namely, that all number theoretical questions are decidable by the human mind—which is too strong to be acceptable. The argument is therefore not convincing. Despite this conclusion, it will be interesting, nevertheless, to give a brief account of Gödel's dualism.

Gödel seems to have devoted considerable effort to studying and trying to answer Turing's arguments on the mind–machine question. In connection with one of these arguments, Gödel spoke to Wang of 'two . . . assumptions, which today are generally accepted, namely: 1 There is no mind separate from matter. 2 The brain functions basically like a digital computer. (2 may be replaced by: 2′ The physical laws, in their observable consequences, have a finite limit of precision.)' (Wang 1974: 236). Wang comments: 'However, while Gödel thinks that 2 is very likely and 2′ practically certain, he believes that 1 is a prejudice of our time, which will be disproved scientifically (perhaps by the fact that there aren't enough nerve cells to perform the observable operations of the mind)' (Wang 1974: 326).

So Gödel thought that the brain functions basically like a digital computer. His argument for this seems to have been that, because of the finite limits of precision in the observable consequences of physical laws, the brain could be regarded as a discrete state machine, and so representable as a Turing machine. It is interesting that Gödel's claim here is stronger than that of Turing, for Turing argued only for the weaker thesis that the operations of the brain could be simulated by a digital computer sufficiently closely for the difference to be undetectable under the conditions of the imitation game. On the other point, however, Gödel diverged strongly from Turing in advocating a Cartesian type of dualism. He even thought that this dualism might be established scientifically by showing that the number of nerve cells in the brain was not sufficient to account for the observable operations of the mind.

In his 1993 paper, Wang gives some further material concerning Gödel's ideas about dualism. Wang reports that on 13 October 1971 Gödel used more or less the following words:

> Even if the finite brain cannot store an infinite amount of information, the spirit may be able to. The brain is a computing machine [situated in the special manner of being] connected with a spirit. If the brain is taken as physical and as a digital computer, from quantum mechanics there are then only a finite number of states. Only by connecting it to a spirit might it work in some other way. (Wang 1993: 127)

Gödel's idea seems to be that the mind's capacity to handle the infinite—e.g. in set theory—shows that it cannot be identified with a finite machine like a brain. Perhaps he believed that this thought could be developed into the scientific proof of dualism which he mentions in the previous passage.

Gödel's strong advocacy of dualism contrasts sharply with the views of Penrose.[6] Penrose uses the Lucas argument[7] to claim that human thinking goes beyond what could be carried out by a computer. As he says:

> It has, indeed, been an underlying theme of the earlier chapters that there seems to be something *non-algorithmic* about our conscious thinking. In particular, a conclusion from the argument in Chapter 4, particularly concerning Gödel's theorem, was that, at least in mathematics, conscious contemplation can sometimes enable one to ascertain the truth of a statement in a way that no algorithm could. (Penrose 1989: 532)

Any procedure carried out by a computer is algorithmic in character. So, if some human thinking—e.g. the thought process by which we see that the Gödel sentence undecidable in S is actually true—is non-algorithmic in character, then human thinking must go beyond what can be achieved by a computer. As Penrose puts it, non-algorithmic thinking, which he regards as the hallmark of consciousness itself, is 'something that the AI people would have no concept of how to program on a computer' (Penrose 1989: 532).

So far Penrose is in agreement with Gödel, and we might expect him to conclude, like Gödel, that human thinking depends on a spiritual mind distinct from the material brain. Penrose, however, takes another, and quite original, line. He regards human thinking as carried out by the material brain, but he postulates that the brain makes use of some physical effects which are not employed by digital computers, and which allow the brain to think non-algorithmically. These physical effects are not a consequence of any of the current theories of physics, and so a new and revolutionary physical theory will be needed to derive them, and hence to explain how the human brain works.

There are, so Penrose argues, reasons internal to physics itself why such a new physical theory is needed. Quantum mechanics generates a whole series of paradoxes which, despite efforts going on for over sixty years, have not been satisfactorily resolved. In particular there is no adequate account of how quantum mechanics at the micro-level meshes with classical physics at the macro-level. Penrose believes that these problems can be resolved only by devising a new theory, and that this new theory will also be needed to explain how the brain works, and, in particular, how non-algorithmic thought is possible. As Penrose himself puts it:

I have made no bones of the fact that I believe that the resolution of the puzzles of quantum theory must lie in our finding an improved theory. . . . We know that at the sub-microscopic level of things the quantum laws do hold sway; but at the level of cricket balls, it is classical physics. Somewhere in between, I would maintain, we need to understand the new law, in order to see how the quantum world merges with the classical. I believe, also, that we shall need this new law if we are ever to understand minds! (Penrose 1989: 385–6)

Penrose also gives the following elegant summary of the main features of his position:

I point out that there could well be room, within physical laws, for an action that is *not algorithmic*—i.e., that cannot be properly simulated by any computer—though I argue that it is likely that such non-algorithmic action can arise only in an area of physics where there is an important gap in our present physical understanding: the no-man's-land between quantum and classical physics. (*Mathematical* processes of a non-algorithmic kind certainly do exist, but the question I am raising is whether such processes have a role to play in *physics*.) I also argue that there is good evidence that conscious thinking is itself not an algorithmic activity, and that consequently the brain must be making use of non-algorithmic physical processes in an essential way whenever consciousness comes into play. There must accordingly be aspects of the brain's action that cannot be properly simulated by the action of a computer, in the sense that we understand the term 'computer' today. (Penrose *et al.* 1990: 643)

Penrose goes on to argue that any properly intelligent entity must be conscious, and so, from his claim that consciousness involves non-algorithmic processes, could not be a computer. Thus the AI project is an illusion, and AI workers are producing 'The Emperor's New Mind'.

Having given an account of the views of Gödel, Lucas, and Penrose on minds and machines, I will now give a brief sketch of my own opinions on this question, and will then spend the remaining three sections of the chapter arguing for these opinions in detail. To begin with, I think that there is no satisfactory argument leading from Gödel's incompleteness theorems to the conclusion that minds are superior to (or at least different from) computers. I have already argued that Gödel's attempt to construct such an argument did not succeed, because the premiss used—i.e. that all number theoretical questions are decidable by the human mind—is too strong to be believable. In the next two sections I will go through objections to the Lucas argument, and argue that these are fatal to the argument (and indeed to Penrose's version of the argument as well). At this point it may seem that I am totally opposed to the views of Gödel, Lucas, and Penrose, but this is not altogether so. Despite differences there are some points of agreement.

First of all I will argue strongly for the thesis that human beings are, and will always remain, superior to computers. However, the character of this superiority is, I will claim, rather different from the way it is imagined by Gödel and Penrose. The superiority in my opinion is one of *power*, or, as it might be put, a *political* superiority. Superiority of this sort does not carry the implication that human beings have minds or brains which can do things that no computer can do. Political superiority is quite compatible, so I will argue, with the mind and the brain being the same, and with each individual human brain being completely representable by a Turing machine, and so, in principle, exactly simulable by a digital computer. There is thus no need to postulate that we have powerful minds separate from our brains, or that our brains make use of some mysterious non-algorithmic physics. I am not, of course, saying that these intriguing speculations are necessarily false, only that they are not needed to explain any features of the relations between human beings and computers.

At this point in the argument, I introduce a Gödel-type argument, but one of a rather different character from those we have been considering hitherto. In a sense I reverse the direction of development. Instead of arguing from Gödel's incompleteness theorems to the superiority of humans over computers, I claim that, just because humans are superior to computers in the political sense, the conditions are appropriate for a Gödel-type argument to be applied. From this argument, and other related considerations, I draw the conclusion that the development of computers and artificial intelligence will never make human thinking superfluous, but, on the contrary, will stimulate human thought to new efforts and achievements. I will also try to show that this conclusion accords well with the advances in artificial intelligence described in the earlier chapters of this book.

Such then is a sketch of the remainder of this chapter. I will now begin the argument by discussing in the next section one of the principal objections to the Lucas argument. This objection, first put forward by Benacerraf (1967), is concerned with possible limitations on human self-knowledge.

6.4. Objections to the Lucas Argument: (i) Possible Limitations on Self-Knowledge

Benacerraf considers the possibility that we are all Turing machines, but each of us is unable to get to know his or her machine table or program. In Lucas's terms, I cannot get to know the formal system which represents me. Since I cannot get to know the formal system, I cannot apply Gödel's method of producing a proposition which is true but unprovable in the system, and thus Lucas's argument fails.

Benacerraf puts the point like this: '*It seems to be consistent with all this that I am indeed a Turing machine, but one with such a complex machine table (program) that I cannot ascertain what it is. In a relevant sense, if I am a Turing machine, then perhaps I cannot ascertain which one*' (1967: 29, emphasis in original). He also adds rather wittily: 'If I am a Turing machine, then I am barred by my very nature from obeying Socrates' profound philosophic injunction: KNOW THYSELF' (Benacerraf 1967: 30).

I have here given an informal account of Benacerraf's argument. In Benacerraf (1967) he develops a much more formal and precise version of the argument. However, in the appendix to the paper he presents a paradox using similar reasoning, and this casts doubts on his earlier conclusions. The problem was taken up by Hanson (1971). Hanson gives a way of avoiding Benacerraf's paradox, but this also blocks Benacerraf's earlier reasoning about mechanism. Chihara, however, shows that (1972: 518): 'Benacerraf's argument can indeed be resuscitated in a system whose syntactical rules conform to Hanson's restrictions and block the derivation of the paradox.' Thus Chihara shows that Benacerraf's formal argument can be developed in a way which is rigorous and free from objections. At the same time, however, Chihara finds some distinctly counter-intuitive features in Benacerraf's argument. As Chihara says:

Benacerraf's own attitude toward his argument is a little puzzling: He refers to his conclusions as 'meager results'. Yet, compared with most 'philosophical results', the conclusions seem—at first sight, anyway—to be so far-reaching and nontrivial as to be counter-intuitive. It is natural to suppose that, if I were a Turing machine, it should be at least theoretically possible to discover its program. How can the considerations advanced by Benacerraf put this sort of limit on the discoveries open to the empirical sciences? (Chihara 1972: 512)

Moreover, Chihara recounts a conversation he had with Paul Grice which draws attention to another curious consequence of the Benacerraf argument:

what the argument shows, at best, is that *I* can never discover 'my own program'. As Paul Grice once remarked to me, 'You may be unable to discover your own program, but that doesn't prevent *me* from discovering your program.' My response to this humorous remark was: 'Yes, but if you do discover my program, you won't be able to tell me what you discover.' This seems to be an absurdity: your not being able to tell me what you discover. And since the absurdity seems to be a consequence of mechanism, one might conclude that mechanism is rendered highly unlikely by this chain of thought. (Chihara 1972: 524)

Chihara does not, however, draw the conclusion that these considerations give any good reasons for rejecting mechanism, but rather presents some arguments, and constructs an interesting example (1972: 524–6), which mitigate the apparently paradoxical features of Grice's point. I agree with Chihara's line of thought here, and will give below some further informal arguments which suggest that the apparently counter-intuitive consequences of Benacerraf's point of view are in reality perfectly natural, and to be expected. The best way of introducing these considerations is by examining in rather more detail how Benacerraf's approach can be used to block the Lucas argument.

In his reply to Benacerraf, Lucas formulates his argument as follows:

A Limit on Artificial Intelligence?

The mechanist—let us grant to Benacerraf that he is no mere man, but the Prince of Darkness himself—produces the specification of a machine which he claims is equivalent to me. From the specification, I calculate the Gödelian formula, and I ask the mechanist (not the machine) whether it is one the machine can prove-in-its-system. . . . If he said that the machine could prove-in-its-system the Gödelian formula, then I should know that the system was inconsistent, and so could not be equivalent to me: while if he said that the machine could not prove-in-its-system the Gödelian formula, then I should know, since there was at least one well-formed formula it could not prove-in-its-system, that it was absolutely consistent and so that the Gödelian formula was true, although the machine could not prove-it-in-its-system, and hence that the machine was not equivalent to me. (Lucas 1968a: 152)

Note that this version of the argument is designed to overcome Putnam's objection about ignorance of the consistency of the system. However, the issue before us now is not Putnam's objection, but Benacerraf's. What step in the above argument might be blocked by Benacerraf's counter-argument? It seems to me to be the following: 'From the specification, I calculate the Gödelian formula . . .'. Suppose, however, I am really the Turing machine specified by the Prince of Darkness. When he presents me with the specification, it might be so complicated that I am quite unable to understand it and to see how the Gödelian formula could be derived. Is there anything implausible or counter-intuitive about such a possibility? Far from being counter-intuitive, it seems to me the kind of outcome which is very natural and to be expected.

To see this, let us return to our earlier example, in which, in an instance of the imitation game, Lucas had to decide which of a concealed Moshé Machover and a concealed computer was the human being. We supposed that Lucas made the wrong decision, but that Moshé Machover then demonstrated his superiority to the computer by calculating the corresponding Gödelian undecidable proposition from the machine specification. As a matter of fact, this example worked only because of the choice of an expert logician for the human being. Suppose we replace Moshé Machover by Mr A, a randomly selected member of the population, it seems almost certain that Mr A would not be able to produce any Gödelian undecidable sentence. It is much more likely that Mr A would never have heard of Gödel, and also be quite unable to understand the machine specification.

Here it might be objected that we might be able to teach Mr A about Gödel's incompleteness theorems, and about machine specifications, and so on. But realistically one has to ask what percentage of the population would ever be able to follow and reproduce a full formal proof of Gödel's incompleteness theorems. Consider a class of mathematics undergraduates doing a course in formal logic. How many, if asked in the examination to reproduce the Gödel–Rosser undecidable sentence for a simple formal system such as 1st-order Peano arithmetic, defining in detail all the terms involved, would be able to do so correctly? Probably 70 per cent is an optimistic estimate, and yet these students are a group already selected for mathematical ability. If now the Devil were to present to even the best students in the class some enormously complicated formal system whose relation to 1st-order Peano arithmetic was far from clear, how many would be able to apply the Gödelian argument to such a system and to formulate correctly a Gödelian undecidable sentence. It does not seem to me at all counter-intuitive to suppose that not a single student would be able to do it. On the contrary, for a sufficiently complicated and devilish formal system that is just what one would expect.

Let us now return to Grice's point that he might get to know Chihara's machine specification, but would be unable to inform Chihara what it was. Is there anything counter-intuitive about *this* situation? It seems to me that there is not. Consider my friend X, the brilliant mathematician. X is always coming into my office to explain his latest curious proof of some deep theorem. The unfortunate thing is that I can never understand his explanations. I am sure that X has grasped the proof, but my limitations as a mathematician mean that he cannot convey it to me. Now suppose, on the mechanist hypothesis, that X and I are both Turing machines, but that X is a more powerful Turing machine than I am. There is nothing contradictory about supposing that X can get to know my machine specification, and hence produce as true a Gödelian proposition which is undecidable for me. There seems to me, however, nothing at all counter-intuitive about my failing to understand both the Gödelian proposition, and X's proof of it. Indeed my regular dealings with X suggest that this would be a quite normal and everyday situation.

Benacerraf's supposition was that each of us might be a Turing machine which is unable to ascertain its own program. I conclude that his supposition is quite coherent, does not have any counter-intuitive consequences, and does indeed block the Lucas argument.

A Limit on Artificial Intelligence?

My reasoning for this conclusion did depend on a consideration of individual limitations. Now Penrose's version of the Lucas argument involves an extension of the argument from the individual to the community. Might this version therefore escape Benacerraf's objection? This is what I will next consider.

Penrose presents his argument as an attempted *reductio ad absurdum* of the supposition that the ways human mathematicians form their conscious judgements of mathematical truth are algorithmic. He writes:

it is one of the most striking features of mathematics (perhaps almost alone among the disciplines) that the truth of propositions can actually be settled by abstract argument! A mathematical argument that convinces one mathematician—providing that it contains no error—will also convince another, as soon as the argument has been fully grasped. . . .

Thus we are not talking about various obscure algorithms that might happen to be running around in different particular mathematicians' heads. We are talking about *one* universally employed formal system which is *equivalent* to *all* the different mathematicians' algorithms for judging mathematical truth. Now this putative 'universal' system, or algorithm, cannot ever be known as the one that we mathematicians use to decide truth! For if it were, then we *could* construct its Gödel proposition and know that to be a mathematical truth also. Thus, we are driven to the conclusion that the algorithm that mathematicians actually use to decide mathematical truth is so complicated or obscure that its very validity can never be known to us.

But this flies in the face of what mathematics is all about! The whole point of our mathematical heritage and training is that we do *not* bow down to the authority of some obscure rules that we can never hope to understand. We must *see*—at least in principle—that each step in the argument can be reduced to something simple and obvious. Mathematical truth is not a horrendously complicated dogma whose validity is beyond our comprehension. It is something built up from such simple and obvious ingredients—and when we comprehend them, their truth is clear and agreed by all.

To my thinking, this is as blatant a *reductio ad absurdum* as we can hope to achieve, short of an actual mathematical proof! The message should be clear. Mathematical truth is *not* something that we ascertain merely by the use of an algorithm. (Penrose 1989: 539–40)

I do not think that Penrose's extension of the Lucas argument from the individual to the community in reality makes the argument any stronger. There are almost certainly mathematical results too difficult for a particular individual to understand and know;

and exactly the same applies to the community of mathematicians as a whole. Thus the postulation of an algorithm too complicated for the human mathematical community to understand is by no means implausible. But does it fly in the face of our mathematical heritage and training to suppose that such an algorithm is being used unconsciously to decide mathematical truth? Do we not, as Penrose claims, decide that a particular step in a mathematical argument is valid, because we 'see' that it is obviously correct? Of course we do indeed decide that the step is valid by 'seeing' that it is obviously correct, *but* that in no way contradicts the supposition that this 'seeing' is based upon the use of an algorithm of which we are quite unaware. To suppose that the two things are in contradiction arises from a failure to distinguish two different levels. If we assume materialism, which seems to be Penrose's position, these two different levels are (1) the conscious stream of thoughts and ideas in the mind of an individual mathematician—Ms B, say, and (2) the corresponding series of electrochemical events, neuronal activity, and so on going on in Ms B's brain, which in some mysterious way give rise to the conscious thoughts and ideas. Now the 'seeing' that a step in a mathematical argument is valid has to be a well-defined event in Ms B's consciousness. This, as Penrose points out, is essential to mathematical activity. However, the brain processes which, on the materialist assumption, give rise to this conscious experience are, of course, completely unknown to Ms B, and this in no way 'flies in the face of what mathematics is all about'.

Indeed, Penrose's own position is that the brain events which give rise to e.g. seeing that the Gödelian sentence is true are not only unknown, but can only be explained by devising some entirely new and, *a fortiori*, completely unknown and unimagined theory of physics. If this does not contradict our mathematical heritage (which it does not), I do not see why the mechanist assumption that the brain processes can be represented by a Turing machine with some extremely complicated and obscure machine table in any way contradicts our mathematical heritage.

Penrose might reply that there is still a difference between the two hypotheses, for his new physical theory might one day be discovered, whereas, on the 'brain = a computer' assumption, the part of the computer's program which underlies mathematical activity must necessarily remain forever unknown. However, it seems to me more plausible that there should be inherent limitations to the extent that the human brain can know itself than that it should be possible for the human brain to understand itself completely.

I conclude, therefore, that Benacerraf's considerations about the possible limitations of self-knowledge do constitute an effective rejoinder both to the original Lucas argument and to Penrose's extension of it. Benacerraf's line of thought is not, however, the only possible way of attacking the Lucas argument. I will consider some further objections to the argument, based on quite different considerations, in the next section.

6.5. Objections to the Lucas Argument: (ii) Possible Additions of Learning Systems

In the Lucas argument, the mechanist thesis is formulated by supposing that a particular mind, Mr A's, say, can be represented by a formal system, S, say. The argument proceeds by applying Gödel's first incompleteness theorem to S. There is here, however, an implicit assumption that the formal system S will be one of the same general kind for which Gödel's incompleteness theorems are proved—that is to say, it is implicitly assumed that S has a fixed set of axioms and that theorems are derived from these axioms by classical logic. The point I want to make next, however, is that, if we really wanted to represent Mr A's mind by a formal system, this system would surely have to be of a rather different character from those which characteristically appear in mathematical books, and for which Gödel's incompleteness theorems are proved. Let us now examine some of these differences.

Into Mr A's mind there constantly enters a stream of new sensations deriving from the external world. The formal system S modelling his mind could not, therefore, have a fixed set of axioms, but would have to be a dynamic system to which new axioms were constantly being added. In terms of the hardware, the machine would have to have sensors allowing a continuous stream of new information. Moreover, in addition to this stream of new axioms corresponding to sensory inputs, the formal system S would have to have inductive rules of inference as well as deductive ones. These inductive rules of inference would enable generalizations to be produced from the new axioms corresponding to sensory input. This is perfectly possible, as we saw from the analysis of machine-learning programs in Chapter 2. However, some of the new generalizations might contradict some of the old ones, and S would have to have some inference rules for resolving such conflicts and perhaps restoring consistency. The AI community is very familiar with the need for formal systems of the type just sketched in order to model learning machines. Formal systems of this kind would certainly be needed to model the human mind, but does the Lucas argument still apply to such systems? I will next argue that it does not.

The new kind of formal system is dynamic in nature and involves inductive and other non-classical rules of inference. It is, therefore, not at all clear that Gödel's method which was developed for static formal systems[8] with classical logic still applies here. Let us suppose, however, that it does still apply to the dynamic system S taken at a particular moment of time t. This will be called S_t. Suppose it is claimed that S is an exact representation of my mind. I consider S_t, and calculate its Gödelian sentence. At time u, where u>t, I triumphantly 'produce-as-true' the Gödelian sentence, p, say, and claim that this shows that I differ from S. The problem with my claim is that the relevant time-slice of S is now S_u, and, although p cannot be proved in S_t, it might well be provable in S_u. Thus the Lucas argument fails.

It might, however, be objected to this line of thought that it can be evaded by the simple expedient of stating the Lucas argument in terms of Turing machines rather than formal systems. Let us take one of the new kind of dynamic formal systems. However complicated the inductive or non-classical rules of inference it employs, they can, provided they are effective, be simulated by a Turing machine. Moreover, the new 'sensory-input' axioms can be simulated by data being added to the input tape of the Turing machine. Thus, whatever the extra complexities involved, we are brought back to a Turing machine. Indeed, a complicated machine-learning system such as GOLEM with its inductive rules of inference and perhaps confirmation SF logic is still run on an ordinary digital computer, which is, of course, a Turing machine. Thus, it could be argued, the consideration of possible additions of learning systems is irrelevant. We simply restate the argument in terms of Turing machines, and the difficulty is avoided.

My reply is that the Lucas argument cannot be carried through entirely in terms of Turing machines. The argument hinges crucially on the human mind being able to produce-as-true a proposition which the machine cannot prove. However, Turing machines can be specified just in terms of numbers and operations on numbers.

A Limit on Artificial Intelligence?

Before we can talk meaningfully of producing-as-true some proposition, a linguistic representation of the Turing machine is clearly necessary, and this will inevitably be a formal system of some kind.

This is the point at which I want to raise some questions about the representability assumption—i.e. the assumption that a Turing machine can be represented as a formal system. Hitherto I have gone along with the tacit supposition that this representability is an unproblematic matter. It is time now to point out that there are some difficulties involved. It might, for example, be possible to represent a Turing machine by a formal system in more than one way. For some such representations—e.g. the dynamic formal systems just considered—Gödel's method might not be directly applicable to the formal system so that the Lucas argument would be blocked in this way. For other such representations, Gödel's method could be applied to the formal system, but the results of the application would not show that the corresponding Turing machine differed from the relevant human mind. Let me next give an example of this second situation.

Suppose a particular Turing machine T is designed to simulate the workings of the brain of Mr A. Mr A's sensory input corresponds to material being written onto the input tape of T. The processing of this information corresponds to T moving from one overall state to the next according to the rules of its machine table. Each overall state of T corresponds to a brain state of Mr A, and the rules of the machine table of T correspond to the neurological processes which take one of Mr A's brain states to the next. Now how could we represent all this by a formal system?

The obvious way of proceeding would be to take a description of the initial state of T as an axiom,[9] to devise rules of inference corresponding to T's machine table so that, if q was inferred from r, then q would be a description of the state of T which immediately followed the state described by r according to T's program. In this formal system, the theorems would describe states reachable by T, or equivalently on the mechanist assumption, possible brain states of Mr A. Let us now suppose that we could apply Gödel's method to the resulting formal system and obtain an undecidable proposition p. What would this mean? It would simply describe a state of Mr A's brain which could never actually occur. Is there any problem about this? None that I can see. p might describe a state of Mr A's brain corresponding to his having a hallucination of a pink rat, and, as a matter of fact, it might not be possible for Mr A ever to have a hallucination of a pink rat. Thus the result would in no way demonstrate that Mr A's mind or brain differed from the Turing machine T.

Against this, it might be objected that p would surely have to be interpreted as saying that it was not provable in the formal system. Of course, a coding yielding such an interpretation would have to be constructed to prove the Gödel result, but this arithmetical interpretation might have nothing to do with the interpretation of p in terms of Mr A's brain or mental states. We might, of course, wish to set up the formal system corresponding to T (and hence Mr A) in such a way that, if an arithmetical proposition was proved in the formal system, this corresponded to Mr A thinking that this arithmetical proposition was true. However, to achieve this, a far more complicated representation of T by a formal system would be necessary than the simple one just given. Such a formal system, if it were indeed possible, might have such a character that Gödel's method could not be applied. Thus, to sum up, if we represent a Turing machine by a simple formal system, Gödel's method may apply but its result will not show that the Turing machine is different from a human mind. If, on the other hand, we represent the Turing machine by a formal system of sufficient complexity to pose problems for the mechanist, there is no guarantee that Gödel's method will apply to the system. In either case, the Lucas argument does not go through.

6.6. Why Advances in Computing are more Likely to Stimulate Human Thinking than to Render it Superfluous

In the last two sections I have criticized the Lucas argument, and its extension by Penrose, and claimed that they do not establish that minds are different from computers. This is obviously rather negative, and in this final section of the chapter I will argue for a more positive thesis. I think that an argument which is Gödel-like, even though not exactly based on Gödel's incompleteness theorems, does tell us something about the relations between humans and computers, and I will now expound this argument.

The first step is to try to establish, independently of any Gödelian considerations, that humans are, and will always remain, superior to computers. I believe that this superiority is real, but rather different in character from the way it is imagined by, for example, Gödel and Penrose. The superiority arises from the fact that computers are designed and built by human beings in order to carry out human purposes. If a computer fails to do what its human controllers want it to do, it will, of course, promptly be switched off and reprogrammed so that it does perform its assigned task correctly. This situation puts humans in a relation of power and dominance *vis-à-vis* computers, and it is this which renders humans superior to computers. Human superiority to computers is, one might say, a *political* superiority.

This kind of superiority is illustrated nicely by Stanley Kubrick's famous 1968 scientific fiction film *2001: A Space Odyssey*. The story was taken from a novel by Arthur C. Clarke, who wrote the screenplay. The second half of the film concerns an expedition to Jupiter in a space ship whose functioning is controlled by a super-intelligent talking computer called HAL.[10] Drama arises because HAL starts to malfunction, and, instead of obeying the orders of the human crew, acts contrary to their interests, even killing some of them. The consequences for HAL are predictable. The member of the crew who remains alive makes his way, despite the obstacles which HAL places in his path, to HAL's central processing unit and shuts it down. Of course such a bizarre computer malfunction as is portrayed in the film for dramatic effect is unlikely to occur in practice. However, what is indeed certain is that any serious malfunction would result in the computer concerned being closed down. Computers have to do what humans tell them or they are eliminated. This is equivalent to describing a power relation in which humans are the masters.

This power relation between humans and computers can be compared to a power relation between different groups of human beings which actually existed at one time. In the Middle Ages, the aristocratic or landlord class had the political relation of superiority to the peasantry. A landlord could order the peasants on his estate to hand over the rent, perform forced labour services, and so on. Any peasant who disobeyed was condignly punished, and even, in extreme cases, eliminated. Of course, this power relation was sometimes interrupted by events such as a peasants' revolt, but, in normal medieval times, it held with full force.

Now the interesting point to note here is that the aristocrats often attributed their real political superiority to some kind of personal superiority. The most standard belief was that their blood was superior to that of the peasants. Hence such phrases as noble blood, blue blood, aristocratic blood, and so on. This belief was taken very seriously and was not just a manner of speaking. Thus Morris Bishop, a leading historian of the Middle Ages, writes: 'Most gentlewomen breast-fed their babies since it was thought that a common nurse's milk would contaminate noble blood. Blanche of Castile, mother of St Louis, found a woman of the court giving suck to a royal infant; she held up the baby by the heels until it vomited' (Bishop 1971: 133).

Of course, we now know that there is no difference between noble blood and any other human blood, but, even if there had been a difference between the nobility and the peasantry in respect of blood or some other physical or mental characteristic, it would have been quite irrelevant to the political power relation between the two groups. It is perfectly possible to imagine a case (and no doubt such cases did sometimes occur) in which a landlord was distinctly feebler both physically and mentally than the vast majority of the peasants on his estate. Still these peasants would have had to have done what he told them, or face the consequences.

The relevance of all this to the human–computer case should be obvious. Gödel and Penrose both argue for human superiority to computers by trying to isolate some peculiarly human personal quality in which humans excel computers. Thus Gödel argues that humans have non-material minds which will enable them to prove mathematical theorems beyond the capability of any possible computer. Penrose argues that human brains have a capacity, based on hitherto undiscovered laws of physics, to perform non-algorithmic operations beyond the capacity of any Turing machine. From the perspective of a political analysis of human superiority to computers, such theories are analogous to those of the medieval aristocrats who attributed their superiority to the peasantry to the possession of noble blood. The mistake in both cases is to attribute what arises from a social relationship[11] to the personal qualities of individuals. The political superiority of humans to computers would in no way be disturbed by computers becoming superior to humans in some aspect or other of thinking. Computers can already perform long division better than any humans, and soon may be able to play chess better than any human, but this does not prevent us being able to switch off a computer whenever we want to do so. The same would continue to apply whatever advances occur in computer technology.

A Limit on Artificial Intelligence?

Penrose assumes at one point that, if computers became superior intellectually to human beings, they would become our rulers. He considers an AI scenario according to which 'computers would have reached the level of "human equivalence"; and they would again be expected to race beyond whatever level we are able to achieve with our relatively puny brains' (Penrose 1994: 34). Of course; Penrose does not think such a scenario is really possible, but significantly he comments that, in such circumstances, 'it would seem that we must resign ourselves to the prospect of a planet ultimately ruled by insentient machines!' (1994: 35). These passages contain the assumption that, if computers were to become superior intellectually to human beings, then they would become rulers of the planet. However, this assumption seems to me incorrect for the reasons just given.

My next move constitutes a kind of reversal of the arguments of Gödel and Penrose. They both argue, though in different ways, from Gödel's incompleteness theorems to human superiority over computers. I want to say that human political superiority to computers shows that a Gödel-like argument can be applied. My argument cannot have as its conclusion that humans are superior to computers, for that is the premiss of the argument. The conclusion of my argument is a different one—namely, that the development of computers will never render human thinking superfluous, but will rather stimulate human thinking to new efforts. It is clear that concern might arise as to whether the development of computers could make human thought unnecessary. If computers become ever more powerful, it might become simpler just to ask a computer for the solution to a problem rather than to try to solve the problem using one's own human mental powers. In the end human thinking might become completely superfluous. Of course, such a situation would not necessarily be unwelcome to everyone. Someone who found thinking a strain might look forward to a future in which the human race amused itself on the beach while all the hard thought was carried out by computers. However, I will not pursue this fantasy further, since the point of my argument is to show that this hypothetical situation could not arise.

Human political superiority to computers arises, so I have argued, because humans design and build computers to carry out human goals. But, since humans design and build computers, it is always possible for humans to survey computers from the outside, and, as I stressed in Section 6.2, this is precisely the condition for

Gödel's argument in the informal sense to apply. Suppose, then, that a computer is designed to solve a set of problems a, b, c, . . . say. The computer will be representable by a formal system, and, by Gödel's argument, problems will arise in this formal system which the computer will not be able to solve, but which will be soluble if the formal system is surveyed from the outside. Note that, since the computer is designed by human beings, there can be no question of the formal system being too complicated for human comprehension, or at least for comprehension by humans using tools such as other computers. Thus the difficulties raised by Benacerraf do not apply. But this shows that, if a computer is designed to solve problems a, b, c, . . ., it is likely to give rise to further problems x, y, z, . . . say, which the computer itself will not be able to solve, and which will require some human thought for their solution.

I should add that I do not mean to base this argument on the specific mathematical details of Gödel's incompleteness theorems, but rather on Gödel's general line of argument in an informal sense. Thus the argument should be taken as a qualitative, informal argument rather than the attempt at a mathematical proof. What I am saying is that, when we design a computer system to solve a set of problems a, b, c, . . ., the fact that *qua* designers we can survey the computer system from the outside makes it likely from general Gödelian considerations that the design process itself will raise a new set of problems x, y, z, . . . which the computer system itself will not be able to solve, but which will need some human thinking for their resolution.

The conclusion drawn from this argument agrees very well with the examples of artificial intelligence given earlier in the book. Let us consider again some of the machine-learning programs such as ID3 or GOLEM. In order for these to work, it is necessary to code in some background knowledge K. If the program discovers some hitherto unknown law or generalization (h, say), this at once poses the problem to the human experts of how h should be integrated with existing knowledge. This integration process calls for human thought, and will perhaps lead to new background knowledge K′ which calls for a modification of the machine-learning program. In this way knowledge advances through a continuous process of human–computer interaction, in which the human contribution, far from being superfluous, plays a vital role. Those working in the machine-learning field will testify with feeling that the area leads to the intensification of human thought, not its elimination.

A Limit on Artificial Intelligence?

Similar conclusions can be drawn from our other example (logic programming). As we saw, attempts to automate theorem-proving were initially based on classical 1st-order logic. When some of the results of this research were used to implement the first logic programming system PROLOG, it turned out that the logic needed to make the system work in practice was not after all classical logic, but a new, and previously unsuspected kind of logic—namely, non-monotonic logic. PROLOG in fact uses a special kind of non-monotonic logic based on a novel kind of negation known as negation-as-failure. The design of PROLOG thus brought to light logical concepts such as non-monotonicity and negation-as-failure which had not previously been considered. Naturally the investigation of these new concepts has proved an interesting and fruitful task for logicians during the last fifteen to twenty years. This is a striking example of an advance in artificial intelligence, far from rendering human thinking superfluous, on the contrary opening up a new, and previously unsuspected, field for human thought to explore.

Thus both our general Gödel-like argument and an analysis of actual examples support our optimistic conclusion that advances in computing and artificial intelligence are more likely to stimulate human thinking than to render it superfluous.

Notes

Chapter 1. The Inductivist Controversy, or Bacon versus Popper

1. To some extent the present chapter is a shortened version of the treatment of the controversy given in Gillies (1993: 3, 72). The account given there is much longer and includes, for example, a discussion of Duhem's contribution, which will not be mentioned here. The present chapter is not, however, simply an extract from this longer work, because its aim is different. Those aspects of the problem which have more connection with artificial intelligence are given more prominence. I have also changed my mind on a number of points. For example, in the 1993 book I argued that *mechanical falsificationism* could be considered as a form of *Baconian induction* (see 1993: 50). I now think that this is incorrect. I will draw attention to these and other divergences from my 1993 treatment as the account proceeds.

2. On other issues, however, Popper's views come closer to Bacon's. I will mention some of these agreements later on.

3. In Gillies (1993) I also considered the example of Fleming's discovery of penicillin. Although this is very interesting, it does not add anything to the AI arguments which I will be developing in the rest of the book, and so it is omitted here.

4. The historical details about Kepler, which are given in this section and later on in the book, are largely taken from the following three detailed accounts of his life and scientific work: Dreyer (1906: 372–412); Koestler (1959: 225–427); Koyré (1961: 117–464).

5. In the earlier treatment of this subject I used the term *creative induction* (Gillies 1993: 48). As I am taking this type of induction to be exclusively human, Donald Michie pointed out to me that this terminology is unfair to computers, which might also be creative. Since I have no wish to discriminate against computers, I have changed the name to *intuitive induction*.

6. The idea of this section came from some very stimulating conversations with Joseph D. Robinson, Professor of Pharmacology at SUNY Health Science Center, Syracuse, when we met at the Glynn Silver Jubilee meeting in October 1990. Robinson pointed out to me that most drugs are discovered by screening, and argued that this raised severe difficulties for a Popperian 'conjectures-and-refutations' account of scientific development. Later he was kind enough to send me material

relating to this and other questions in philosophy of science. This included the following quotation from Goth, 'most new drugs are discovered today by screening' (1970: 36), on which Joseph Robinson commented that what this does not emphasize is that, for whatever purpose a compound is synthesized, it is put through *all* the screens to see what 'other' activities it may have. This indicates that the discovery of the sulphonamide drugs is quite typical of drug discovery in general, so that the analysis of this case is indeed significant for the study of scientific method.

7. The following account of the 'dye heuristic' used by Domagk was suggested to me by my colleague Melvin Earles, who also lent me his copy of Ehrlich (1906). Some comments from Professor W. C. Bowman of the Department of Physiology and Pharmacology at the University of Strathclyde were also useful.

8. This view is different from the one expressed in Gillies (1993: 50). The reasons for this change of opinion are contained in the rest of the paragraph.

9. It was objected (by an anonymous referee) that this definition of induction is somewhat restrictive, and that one might define induction more generally as consisting of inductive inferences in which the premises support (or purport to support) the conclusion without entailing it. In this case there would be no requirement for a 'mass' of data, and a hypothesis might be inferred inductively from a single piece of data. This could be done, for example, by making an inference to the best explanation of the piece of data.

The term 'induction' is, of course, rather vague, and the broader definition of induction just described might indeed be useful for some purposes. For the present discussion, however, I prefer the narrower definition given in the text, since it seems to characterize the notion of induction used by both Bacon and Popper, and is also, as we shall see, appropriate for considering machine learning.

Chapter 2. Machine Learning in the Turing Tradition

1. Rather than attempt a general explanation of machine learning at this introductory stage, I think it is better to allow the nature of the field to emerge from the examples which will be given in detail later.

2. For those interested in other approaches to machine learning, an excellent survey is to be found in Hutchinson (1994). Hutchinson covers several methods which will not be discussed in this book, e.g. neural nets and Boltzmann machines.

3. Ehud Shapiro's book was drawn to my attention by Stephen Muggleton, to whom I am grateful for several other references concerned

with machine learning, as well as for many helpful conversations about the character of machine learning and its historical development. Many of the ideas of this chapter had their origin in these conversations.

4. For historical details, see Gillies (1982, 1992*c*).

5. See Gillies (1992*a*, 1993: 69–72). There has been a shift in my own opinions from the 1992*a* article to the present. In Gillies (1992*a*) I was rather sceptical about the value of machine learning. The article was in fact written in the summer of 1990, when I had studied the work of Simon and his group but very little of the work done in the Turing tradition. Later that year I began participation in the Rule-Based Systems project, which started in the autumn of 1990. This made me aware of the progress in machine learning of Stephen Muggleton and his group at the Turing Institute in Glasgow, who were involved in the project. The importance of this work 'in the Turing tradition' is acknowledged in Gillies (1993: 71), and its implications for philosophy of science are explored in the present book.

   As my attitude to Simon and his group is highly critical and perhaps unfair, the reader may be interested in seeing a defence of the position by Simon himself. Such a defence is to be found in *International Studies in the Philosophy of Science*, 6/1 (1992). This is a special issue of the journal devoted to the question. It contains an article by Simon (1992), a series of papers commenting on this article (including Gillies 1992*a*), and Simon's reply to his critics.

6. Good accounts of expert systems are to be found in Michie (1982) and Jackson (1986).

7. Feigenbaum (1977) is a report of the Stanford Computer Science Department. The quotation has actually been taken from Quinlan (1979: 168).

8. A similar conclusion was reached by my collaborators and me in connection with our attempt to implement an expert system for colon endoscopy. We wrote: 'As far as possible only qualitative suggestions should be sought from the domain expert, and it should be left to the computer scientist to give this a more precise quantitative form' (Sucar, Gillies, and Gillies 1993: 188). This point was not made in order to advocate the use of machine-learning techniques, but rather to advocate the use of objective probabilities instead of subjective probabilities elicited from domain experts. The problem of which interpretation of probability is appropriate for expert systems will not be further discussed in the present book, but it is interesting to note that the use of objective probabilities, and the use of machine-learning techniques, lead to similar conclusions regarding the role of domain experts.

9. The exact definition of clause is not needed to follow the informal account given here. However, the reader who is familiar with mathematical logic and would like to study the technical details can find a

brief summary of the clausal form of logic in Muggleton (1992: 23–4). This would suffice for such a reader to understand the technical results on which GOLEM is based, and which are contained in Muggleton and Feng (1992: 281–98).

10. At the time of writing (April 1994), Muggleton is working on the development of a new relational learning system (PROGOL), which will be able to make direct use of background knowledge in the form of laws and generalizations.

11. My colleague Richard Sorabji did, however, point out to me that Democritus's concept of cause (*aitiologia*) was almost certainly different from the modern concept of causal law. Greek philosophers of the classical period did not connect cause with law in any way. The Stoics were the first to link cause with exceptionless regularity, but their concept of exceptionless regularity was still different from the modern concept of a scientific law. For details see Sorabji (1980: ch. 3, esp. 60–7).

Chapter 3. How Advances in Machine Learning Affect the Inductivist Controversy

1. Urbach gives arguments for this conclusion throughout his 1987 book, but see particularly ch. 6, sects. vii to ix, pp. 178–85. Although disagreeing with Urbach on this point, I have found his book very helpful in preparing my own account of Bacon. I do, moreover, accept many of Urbach's conclusions, as the next paragraph shows.

2. This passage is cited in Urbach (1987: 183), which drew my attention to it.

3. This was suggested to me by Stephen Muggleton.

4. For more details concerning this theme, see Vernon Pratt's interesting (1987).

Chapter 4. Logic Programming and a New Framework for Logic

1. The account of the development of PROLOG in Section 4.1 is based on a study of the original papers, on useful conversations with Bob Kowalski and Stephen Muggleton, and on Kowalski's 1988 memoir.

2. Of course PROLOG is by no means the only non-monotonic logic, and it is no coincidence that the development of PROLOG in the 1970s was followed by the study of a variety of systems of non-monotonic

logic in the 1980s. Different systems of non-monotonic logic were proposed by McCarthy (1980), McDermott and Doyle (1980), and Reiter (1980). These three papers all appeared in the same issue of the journal *Artificial Intelligence*. Another interesting system was suggested by Nute (1986), while recently Gabbay has brought all these systems (and other non-classical logics used in artificial intelligence) into the general framework of what he calls 'Labelled Deductive Systems' (see Gabbay 1991). We will be discussing some aspects of Gabbay (1991, 1993) later on. As these are research reports, it should be added that revised versions of the material will soon be published in a more widely accessible form. An expanded version of Gabbay (1991) will appear as a book of the same title published by Oxford University Press, while a revised version of Gabbay (1993) will be published in volume ii of the Handbook of Logic in Artificial Intelligence and Logic Programming (Oxford University Press).

3. This example is a variant of one which was given to me by Murray Shanahan.

4. I would like to thank Moshé Machover for suggesting the consideration of Gödel's translations in this context—a suggestion which led to my writing Section 4.3.

5. In quoting from Heyting I have replaced his German letters by bold letters.

6. Moshé Machover pointed out to me that the claim that PROLOG introduced control into deductive logic for the first time needs to be somewhat qualified by the fact the control considerations are involved in the proof of some of the meta-theorems of classical logic. Thus, for example, in the completeness proofs for tableaux in 1st-order classical logic, what are in effect control instructions for the construction of tableaux have to be specified in the course of the meta-level proof. For details, see Bell and Machover (1977: 33–4, 88–93).

7. For a good recent account of Jevons's work in logic, see Schabas (1990: 57–65), while Jevons's logical piano is described and depicted in Pratt (1987: 131–5). Jevons is an important, but hitherto somewhat neglected figure in the history of logic. His logical piano used a method not unlike Robinson's resolution principle. Jevons was also interested in the problem of mechanizing induction, and he anticipated some of the ideas of inductive logic programming.

8. Many of the points about PROLOG in the following paragraphs have been made (sometimes using the same examples) by Cellucci (1993: 213–15). Cellucci's point of view in this paper is similar to the one in this chapter, but, at the same time, more general. Cellucci argues that traditional mathematical logic now needs to be replaced by computational logic. Mathematical logic is connected with the axiomatic method, while the new logic should be related to what he calls the *analytic*

method. In this chapter I am attempting the more limited goal of exploring the differences between classical logic and the logic of PROLOG. I believe that this more circumscribed task can be brought within Cellucci's more general framework of computational logic and the analytic method, with which I find myself in complete sympathy.

9. There are, of course, a number of different versions of PROLOG. The examples given in this book use OU PROLOG which has an Edinburgh-Syntax PROLOG interpreter.

Chapter 5. Can there be an Inductive Logic?

1. Popper prefers to call his theory *corroboration theory* in order to distinguish it from Carnap's *confirmation theory*. The majority of subsequent writers on the subject have not, however, made this distinction, but have used the terms *corroboration* and *confirmation* as synonyms. I will follow the majority in this respect. This is not, of course, to deny that there is a difference between Carnap's theory and Popper's, but to express it in a different way, by saying that Carnap is a Bayesian, and Popper a non-Bayesian.

2. For the interested and technically knowledgeable reader who would like to pursue these issues further, I will list a few recent papers. An attempt to discuss inductive rules of inference in general logical terms is to be found in Cussens and Hunter (1993). I can also mention two recent investigations of the relation between machine learning and confirmation. One of these, which adopts a Bayesian (and even pseudo-Bayesian!) point of view is Cussens (1993). The other, which adopts a non-Bayesian point of view developed from Popper's ideas, is Gillies (1992*b*). It should be stressed that these papers have a preliminary character, and considerable advances in this field over the next decade or so are to be expected.

3. Note that because alpha(X) and not_alpha(X) are treated in the GOLEM with PROLOG approach as two unrelated predicates, not(alpha(X)) is *not* identified with not_alpha(X), nor not(not_alpha(X)) with alpha(X). The alpha rules and the not_alpha rules are used separately, and so given distinct lines in Tables 5.1 and 5.2. As we shall see, alpha(X) and not_alpha(X) are, by contrast, used together in the GOLEM with SF confirmation logic approach.

4. Although these are strong arguments for the empiricist view of logic, they are not, of course, decisive, and counter-arguments could be produced. One such, suggested by an anonymous referee, is the following. Classical logic is the study of truth-preserving inference, and, as such, is universal. It is what we use if we want our arguments to have the following conditional property: if the premises are true, the conclusion

must be true. Of course, there may be situations in which we do not want this conditional property to hold, and, in such situations, other systems such as PROLOG may be appropriate. However, given that we do want this conditional property, the validity of classical logic is clear *a priori*.

My answer to this argument is that it is far from clear that the rules of classical logic do preserve truth. Brouwer, for example, denied that they did preserve truth in mathematics (see his 1908). He regarded a mathematical proposition as true if it described a construction which it was known how to carry out. On this account of truth, it is possible to start with a set of true mathematical propositions, and, by applying the rules of classical logic, including the law of excluded middle, to arrive at conclusions which are no longer true.

Brouwer's argument shows that it is doubtful whether the truth-preserving character of classical logic can be established *a priori*. My own view is that the empirical success in physics of classical mathematics based on classical logic gives empirical support to the truth-preserving character of classical logic *in that area*.

Naturally a great deal more could be said regarding the controversy between the empirical and *a priori* views of logic. In this book I have concentrated on those aspects of the controversy which relate to recent advances in artificial intelligence.

Chapter 6. Do Gödel's Incompleteness Theorems Place a Limit on Artificial Intelligence?

1. I am most grateful to an expert in computer chess—Don Beal of the Department of Computing, Queen Mary College, University of London—for supplying me with the information given in the rest of this paragraph.
2. Kasparov did, however, restore human honour by defeating 'Pentium Genius' in a return match on 20 May 1995. The *Independent on Sunday* reported the next day that Kasparov 'looked mightily relieved when it was all over'.
3. Russell and Whitehead omitted to formalize the rules of inference they were using, but this gap in their formalization can easily be closed, turning *PM* into a fully formalized system.
4. The difference between Gödel's original version of the theorem and the Gödel–Rosser theorem will be explained later on.
5. The history of the Lucas argument is somewhat complicated. Turing states something like the argument as the third objection (which he calls '*The Mathematical Objection*') to his main thesis about machines being able to play the imitation game (1950: 15–16). Turing, however,

quickly dismisses the objection. I will suggest later that one possible reason for his not taking the argument very seriously is that it does not have much force in the context of Turing's imitation game. A form of the argument was also stated by Putnam (1961: 77). However, Putnam, far from defending the argument, claimed that it 'is simply a mistake' (1961: 77). In fact Lucas and Putnam had met in Princeton in 1957, and had each by that time formulated the argument, and adopted their respective attitudes towards it. This naturally meant that they argued about the matter. Lucas has written (private communication) that his discussions with Putnam helped him to develop some of the lines of thought in his 1961 paper.

Gödel also considered the implications of his incompleteness theorems for mechanism, and, like Lucas, concluded that they showed mechanism to be false. However, Gödel's argument is somewhat different from Lucas's, and was published for the first time by Wang in 1974 (Wang 1974: 324–6). Lucas was, therefore, the first to develop the argument in detail and defend it in print. So it seems to me just to refer to it by his name. Since the publication of Lucas (1961), there have been many replies, to which Lucas has in turn replied. I will discuss some of these exchanges in what follows. Lucas presents a further account of his argument, together with some of his answers to objections (1970: 124–72). Here the argument is particularly connected to the issue of determinism.

6. Penrose states his views in Penrose (1989). This led to a discussion in *Behavioral and Brain Sciences*, vol. 13 (1990), and Penrose clarifies his views in his reply to his critics. He elaborates and develops them further in Penrose (1994).

7. This statement is somewhat inaccurate, for, although Penrose's argument is very similar to Lucas's, it differs in some respects. Penrose writes: 'Only a very few of my critics appear even to have noticed that my argument is not the same as that of Lucas (1961)' (Penrose *et al.* 1990: 693). I will describe in the next section (6.4) the changes made by Penrose to the argument.

8. The distinction made here between *static* and *dynamic* systems is, I think, the same as that which Cellucci (1993) draws between *closed* and *open* systems. Cellucci characterizes closed systems as those for which 'their rules are given once for all and allow us to deal only with knowledge not changing in time', and open systems as those for which 'their rules can change at any stage and allow us to deal with knowledge changing in time' (1993: 206). Chihara (1972) also analyses the significance of knowledge changing in time.

9. I am here ignoring the difficulty caused by the fact that new information is being written on the Turing machine's tape all the time corresponding to a flow of sensory information. This simplification is for

the sake of the argument, since taking account of this difficulty can only strengthen my general case.

10. Arthur C. Clarke and Stanley Kubrick apparently consulted some of the leading AI experts of the day, notably Marvin Minsky, about the attributes to be given to the fictional computer HAL. It is worth noting that HAL would certainly be capable of passing the Turing test, and is supposed to exist in the year 2001, almost exactly fifty years after Turing's 1950 paper. It will be recalled that Turing claimed in that paper that fifty years should be sufficient for creating a computer capable of playing his imitation game. Of course, the film is primarily a subtle work of fiction and contains many hidden ironies. The humans in the film act in a mechanical, almost robotic, fashion, while the only really human character is, of course, the computer HAL, which is vain, emotional, neurotic, and so on.

11. I am here using 'social relationship' in a somewhat extended sense to include not just relationships between human beings, but also relationships between human beings and their artefacts, in this case computers.

References

Bacon, F. (1620), *Novum Organum*, Eng. trans. in R. L. Ellis and J. Spedding (eds.), *The Philosophical Works of Francis Bacon* (Routledge, 1905), 212–387.

Bell, J. L., and Machover, M. (1977), *A Course in Mathematical Logic* (North-Holland).

Benacerraf, P. (1967), 'God, the Devil and Gödel', *Monist*, 51: 9–32.

Bishop, M. (1971), *The Penguin Book of the Middle Ages*.

Boyer, R. S., and Moore, J. S. (1972), 'The Sharing of Structure in Theorem-Proving Programs', in B. Meltzer and D. Michie (eds.), *Machine Intelligence 7* (Edinburgh University Press), 101–16.

Branden, C., and Tooze, J. (1991), *Introduction to Protein Structure* (Garland Publishing).

Brouwer, L. E. J. (1908), 'The Unreliability of the Logical Principles', in *Collected Works*, i (North-Holland, 1975), 107–11.

Bratko, I. (1986), *Prolog Programming for Artificial Intelligence* (Addison-Wesley, 1988 repr.).

—— (1992), 'Applications of Machine Learning: Towards Knowledge Synthesis', in *Proceedings of the International Conference on Fifth Generation Computer Systems 1992, Tokyo, Japan* (Institute for New Generation Computer Technology), ii. 1207–18.

Buchanan, B. G., and Feigenbaum, E. A. (1978), 'DENDRAL and Meta-DENDRAL: Their Applications Dimension', *Artificial Intelligence*, 11: 5–24.

Buchanan, B. G., and Mitchell, T. M. (1978), 'Model-Directed Learning of Production Rules', in D. A. Waterman and F. Hayes-Roth (eds.), *Pattern Directed Inference Systems* (Academic Press).

Carnap, R. (1950), *Logical Foundations of Probability* (2nd edn., University of Chicago Press, 1963).

Cellucci, C. (1993), 'From Closed to Open Systems', *Philosophy of Mathematics, Proceedings of the 15th International Wittgenstein Symposium, Part I* (Johannes Czermak), 206–20.

Chihara, C. S. (1972), 'On Alleged Refutations of Mechanism using Gödel's Incompleteness Results', *Journal of Philosophy*, 69: 507–26.

Clark, K. (1978), 'Negation as Failure', in H. Gallaire and J. Minker (eds.), *Logic and Data Bases* (Plenum Press), 293–322.

Cohen, P. J. (1966), *Set Theory and the Continuum Hypothesis* (Benjamin).

Colmerauer, A., Kanoui, H., Pasero, R., and Roussel, P. (1973), 'Un système de communication homme-machine en Français', Research Report, Groupe d'Intelligence Artificielle, Université d'Aix-Marseille II, Luminy.

References

Cussens, J. (1993), 'Bayes and Pseudo-Bayes Estimates of Conditional Probability and their Reliability', in *European Conference on Machine Learning (ECML-93)* (Springer-Verlag), 136–52.

Cussens, J., and Hunter, A. (1993), 'Towards a Logical Analysis of Inductive Learning', Research Report, Department of Computing, Imperial College, University of London.

Cussens, J., Hunter, A., and Srinivasan, A. (1993), 'Generating Explicit Orderings for Non-monotonic Logics', *Proceedings of the 11th National Conference on Artificial Intelligence (AAAI-93)* (MIT Press), 420–5.

Davis, R., Buchanan, B. G., and Shortliffe, E. H. (1977), 'Production Systems as a Representation for a Knowledge-Based Consultation Program', *Artificial Intelligence*, 8: 15–45.

Dolšak, B., and Muggleton, S. (1992), 'The Application of Inductive Logic Programming to Finite-Element Mesh Design', in Stephen Muggleton (ed.), *Inductive Logic Programming* (Academic Press), 453–72.

Dreyer, J. L. E. (1906), *A History of Astronomy from Thales to Kepler* (Dover edn., 1953).

Dreyfus, H. L. (1972), *What Computers Can't Do: A Critique of Artificial Reason* (Harper & Row).

Dummett, M. A. E. (1973), 'The Philosophical Basis of Intuitionistic Logic', repr. in Michael Dummett, *Truth and Other Enigmas* (Duckworth, 1978), 215–47.

—— (1977), *Elements of Intuitionism* (Oxford University Press).

Džeroski, S., and Bratko, I. (1992), 'Handling Noise in Inductive Logic Programming', *International Workshop on Inductive Logic Programming (ILP92)*, ed. S. Muggleton and K. Furukawa, ICOT Technical Memorandum: TM-1182, 109–25.

Ehrlich, P. (1906), 'Address Delivered at the Dedication of the Georg-Speyer-Haus', repr. in Eng. trans. in L. Shuster (ed.), *Readings in Pharmacology* (Churchill, 1962), 233–43.

Feigenbaum, E. A. (1977), 'The Art of Artificial Intelligence: 1 Themes and Case Studies of Knowledge Engineering', Computer Science Department Report STAN-CS-77-621, Stanford University, Stanford, California.

Freeman, K. (1947), *Ancilla to the Pre-Socratic Philosophers* (6th impression, Blackwell, 1971).

Frege, G. (1879), *Begriffsschrift, Eine der arithmetischen nachgebildete Formelsprache des reinen Denkens*, Eng. trans. in Jean van Heijenoort (ed.), *From Frege to Gödel: A Source Book in Mathematical Logic, 1879–1931* (Harvard University Press, 1977), 1–82.

—— (1880–1), 'Boole's Logical Calculus and the Concept-Script', Eng. trans. in *Gottlob Frege: Posthumous Writings* (Blackwell), 9–52.

—— (1884), *The Foundations of Arithmetic: A Logico-Mathematical Enquiry into the Concept of Number*, English trans. by J. L. Austin (Blackwell, 1968).

Gabbay, D. M. (1991), 'Labelled Deductive Systems. Part I', Technical report,

References

CIS-Bericht-90-22, Centrum für Informations- und Sprachverarbeitung, Universität München.

—— (1993), 'Classical vs Non-classical Logics: The Universality of Classical Logic', Technical Report, MPI-I-93-230, Max-Planck-Institut für Informatik, Im Stadtwald, Saarbrücken.

Gillies, D. A. (1982), *Frege, Dedekind, and Peano on the Foundations of Arithmetic* (Van Gorcum).

—— (1987), 'Was Bayes a Bayesian?', *Historia Mathematica*, 14: 325–46.

—— (1990), 'The Turing–Good Weight of Evidence Function and Popper's Measure of the Severity of a Test', *British Journal for the Philosophy of Science*, 41: 143–6.

—— (1992a), 'Comments on "Scientific Discovery as Problem Solving" by Herbert A. Simon', *International Studies in the Philosophy of Science*, 6: 29–31.

—— (1992b), 'Confirmation Theory and Machine Learning', *International Workshop on Inductive Logic Programming (ILP2)*, ed. S. Muggleton and K. Furukawa, ICOT Technical Memorandum: TM-1182, 40–51.

—— (1992c), 'The Fregean Revolution in Logic', in Donald Gillies (ed.), *Revolutions in Mathematics* (Oxford University Press), 265–305.

—— (1993), *Philosophy of Science in the Twentieth Century: Four Central Themes* (Blackwell).

Gödel, K. (1931), 'On Formally Undecidable Propositions of *Principia Mathematica* and Related Systems I', repr. with German original and English translation in *Collected Works*, i (Oxford University Press, 1986), 144–95.

—— (1933), 'On Intuitionistic Arithmetic and Number Theory', repr. with German original and English translation in *Collected Works*, i (Oxford University Press, 1986), 286–95.

—— (1940), *The Consistency of the Continuum Hypothesis* (Princeton University Press).

—— (1963), 'What is Cantor's continuum problem?', reprint of the 1963 revision of a 1947 paper in Paul Benacerraf and Hilary Putnam (eds.), *Philosophy of Mathematics: Selected Readings* (2nd edn., Cambridge University Press, 1983), 470–85.

Goth, A. (1970), *Medical Pharmacology* (C. V. Mosby).

Grosholz, E. (1992), 'Was Leibniz a Mathematical Revolutionary?', in Donald Gillies (ed.), *Revolutions in Mathematics* (Oxford University Press), 117–33.

Hanson, W. (1971), 'Mechanism and Gödel's Theorems', *British Journal for the Philosophy of Science*, 22: 9–16.

Hayes, P. J. (1973), 'Computation and Deduction', in *Proceedings of the 2nd MFCS Symposium* (Czechoslovakian Academy of Sciences), 105–18.

Heyting, A. (1956), *Intuitionism: An Introduction* (2nd rev. edn., North-Holland, 1966).

Hodges, A. (1983), *Alan Turing: The Enigma of Intelligence* (Unwin Paperback, 1987).

Hunt, E. B., Marin, J., and Stone, P. J. (1966), *Experiments in Induction* (Academic Press).

Hutchinson, A. (1994), *Algorithmic Learning* (Oxford University Press).

Jackson, P. (1986), *Introduction to Expert Systems* (Addison-Wesley).

Jevons, W. S. (1870), 'On the Mechanical Performance of Logical Inference', *Philosophical Transactions of the Royal Society*, 160: 497–518.

—— (1874), *The Principles of Science* (London: Macmillan).

Koestler, A. (1959), *The Sleepwalkers: A History of Man's Changing Vision of the Universe* (Pelican edn., 1968).

Kowalski, R. A. (1974), 'Predicate Logic as a Programming Language', in Jack L. Rosenfeld (ed.), *Information Processing 74, Proceedings of IFIP Congress 74 Organised by the International Federation for Information Processing. Stockholm, Sweden, August 5–10* (North-Holland), 569–74.

—— (1979a), 'Algorithm Equals Logic Plus Control', *Communications of the ACM (Association for Computing Machinery)*, 22/7: 424–36.

—— (1979b), *Logic for Problem Solving* (North-Holland).

—— (1988), 'The Early Years of Logic Programming', *Communications of the ACM (Association for Computing Machinery)*, 31/1: 38–43.

Kowalski, R. A., and Kuehner, D. (1971), 'Linear Resolution with Selection Function', *Artificial Intelligence*, 2: 227–60.

Koyré, A. (1961), *The Astronomical Revolution: Copernicus–Kepler–Borelli*, Eng. trans. by R. E. W. Maddison (Methuen, 1973).

Langley, P., Simon, H. A., Bradshaw, G. L., and Zytkow, J. M. (1987), *Scientific Discovery: Computational Explorations of the Creative Processes* (MIT Press).

Loveland, D. W. (1969), 'A Simplified Format for the Model-Elimination Theorem-Proving Procedure', *Journal of the Association for Computing Machinery*, 16: 349–63.

Lucas, J. R. (1961), 'Minds, Machines, and Gödel', repr. in Alan Ross Anderson (ed.), *Minds and Machines* (Prentice-Hall, 1964), 43–59.

—— (1968a), 'Satan Stultified: A Rejoinder to Paul Benacerraf', *Monist*, 52: 145–58.

—— (1968b), 'Human and Machine Logic: A Rejoinder', *British Journal for the Philosophy of Science*, 19: 155–6.

—— (1970), *The Freedom of the Will* (Oxford University Press).

McCarthy, J. (1980), 'Circumscription—a Form of Non-Monotonic Reasoning', *Artificial Intelligence*, 13: 27–39.

McDermott, D., and Doyle, J. (1980), 'Non-Monotonic Logic I', *Artificial Intelligence*, 13: 41–72.

Mendelson, E. (1964), *Introduction to Mathematical Logic* (Van Nostrand).

Meyerson, E. (1908), *Identity and Reality*, Eng. trans. Kate Loewenberg (2nd impression, Allen and Unwin, 1964).

References

Michalski, R. S., and Chilautsky, R. L. (1980), 'Learning by Being Told and Learning from Examples: An Experimental Comparison of the Two Methods of Knowledge Acquisition in the Context of Developing an Expert System for Soybean Disease Diagnosis', *Journal of Policy Analysis and Information Systems*, 4: 125–61.

Michie, D. (1982) (ed.), *Introductory Readings in Expert Systems* (Gordon and Breach Science Publishers).

Mueller, R. A., and Page, R. L. (1988), *Symbolic Computing with Lisp and Prolog* (John Wiley).

Muggleton, S. (1988), 'A Strategy for Constructing New Predicates in First Order Logic', in D. Sleeman (ed.), *Proceedings of the Third European Working Session on Learning* (Pitman), 123–30.

—— (1992), 'Inductive Logic Programming', in Stephen Muggleton (ed.), *Inductive Logic Programming* (Academic Press), 3–27.

Muggleton, S., and Feng, C. (1992), 'Efficient Induction of Logic Programs' in S. Muggleton (ed.), *Inductive Logic Programming* (Academic Press), ch. 13, pp. 281–98.

Muggleton, S., King, R. D., and Sternberg, M. J. E. (1992), 'Protein Secondary Structure Prediction using Logic-Based Machine Learning', *Protein Engineering*, 5/7: 647–57.

Nute, D. (1986), 'LDR: A Logic for Defeasible Reasoning', ACMC Research Report 01-0013, University of Georgia, Athens.

Penrose, R. (1989), *The Emperor's New Mind* (Vintage Paperback Edition, 1990).

—— et al. (1990), 'Discussion of *The Emperor's New Mind*', *Behavioral and Brain Sciences*, 13: 643–705.

—— (1994), *Shadows of the Mind: A Search for the Missing Science of Consciousness* (Oxford University Press).

Plotkin, G. D. (1970), 'A Note on Inductive Generalisation', in B. Meltzer and D. Michie (eds.), *Machine Intelligence, 5* (Elsevier North-Holland), 153–63.

—— (1971*a*), 'Automatic Methods of Inductive Inference', Ph.D. thesis, Edinburgh University.

—— (1971*b*), 'A Further Note on Inductive Generalisation', in B. Meltzer and D. Michie (eds.), *Machine Intelligence, 6* (Elsevier North-Holland), 101–24.

Popper, K. R. (1934), *The Logic of Scientific Discovery*, 6th rev. impression of the 1959 Eng. trans. (Hutchinson, 1972).

—— (1963), *Conjectures and Refutations: The Growth of Scientific Knowledge* (Routledge & Kegan Paul).

Pratt, V. (1987), *Thinking Machines: The Evolution of Artificial Intelligence* (Blackwell).

Putnam, H. (1961), 'Minds and Machines', repr. in Alan Ross Anderson (ed.), *Minds and Machines* (Prentice-Hall, 1964), 72–97.

Quine, W. V. O. (1951), 'Two Dogmas of Empiricism' repr. in *From a Logical Point of View* (2nd rev. edn., Harper Torchbooks, 1961), 20–46.

Quinlan, J. R. (1979), 'Discovering Rules by Induction from Large Collections of Examples', in Donald Michie (ed.), *Expert Systems in the Micro-Electronic Age* (Edinburgh University Press), 168–201.

—— (1982), 'Semi-Autonomous Acquisition of Pattern-Based Knowledge', in Donald Michie (ed.), *Introductory Readings in Expert Systems* (Gordon and Breach Science Publishers), 192–207.

—— (1986), 'Induction of Decision Trees', *Machine Learning*, 1: 81–106.

—— (1990), 'Learning Logical Definitions from Relations', *Machine Learning*, 5: 239–66.

Reiter, R. (1971), 'Two Results on Ordering for Resolution with Merging and Linear Format', *Journal of the Association for Computing Machinery*, 15: 630–46.

—— (1980), 'A Logic for Default Reasoning', *Artificial Intelligence*, 13: 81–132.

Robinson, J. A. (1965), 'A Machine-Oriented Logic Based on the Resolution Principle', *Journal of the Association for Computing Machinery*, 12: 23–41.

Rosser, J. B. (1936), 'Extensions of Some Theorems of Gödel and Church', *Journal of Symbolic Logic*, 1: 87–91.

Schabas, M. (1990), *A World Ruled by Number: William Stanley Jevons and the Rise of Mathematical Economics* (Princeton University Press).

Shapiro, E. Y. (1983), *Algorithmic Program Debugging* (MIT Press).

Simon, H. A. (1992), 'Scientific Discovery as Problem Solving', *International Studies in the Philosophy of Science*, 6: 3–14.

Sorabji, R. R. K. (1980), *Necessity Cause and Blame: Perspectives on Aristotle's Theory* (Duckworth).

Srinivasan, A., Muggleton, S., and Bain, M. (1994), 'The Justification of Logical Theories Based on Data Compression', in K. Furukawa, D. Michie, and S. Muggleton (eds.), *Machine Intelligence 13* (Oxford University Press), 87–121.

Sucar, L. E., Gillies, D. F., and Gillies, D. A. (1993), 'Objective Probabilities in Expert Systems', *Artificial Intelligence*, 61: 187–208.

Tennant, N. W. (1978), *Natural Logic* (Edinburgh University Press).

Turing, A. (1936–7), 'On Computable Numbers with an Application to the Entscheidungsproblem', *Proceedings of the London Mathematical Society*, 42: 230–65, 43: 544–6.

—— (1950), 'Computing Machinery and Intelligence', repr. in Alan Ross Anderson (ed.), *Minds and Machines* (Prentice Hall, 1964), 4–30.

Urbach, P. (1987), *Francis Bacon's Philosophy of Science: An Account and a Reappraisal* (Open Court).

Wang, H. (1974), *From Mathematics to Philosophy* (Routledge & Kegan Paul).

—— (1993), 'On Physicalism and Algorithmism: Can Machines Think?', *Philosophia Mathematica*, 1: 97–138.

Index

Index

Index

006.3   Gillies, Donald,
GIL   1944-

         Artificial
          intelligence and
          scientific method.

                    33035000421484

$29.95